Common American Idioms

A Dictionary of the Most Popular American Expressions, with Etymology and Examples

MyEnglishRoutine.com

TABLE OF CONTENTS

TABLE OF CONTENTS

INTRODUCTION

Have you ever wondered if it really rained cats and dogs in Medieval England? Do you think that you can fit an elephant inside the room? Or how does a Cheshire cat smile?

These bizarre questions are some of the expressions that are often used in the English language. Idioms, also known as idiomatic expressions, are expressions that we shouldn't really take literally. Believe it or not, you and I know that we use such expressions on a day to day basis. However, it never occurred to us how these expressions came to be.

The American Idiom is a compilation of idiomatic expressions that have been used in speaking and writing. It contains more than 900 selected idioms with their eccentric origins. We aim to pull out all stops to help you learn some of the daily idiomatic expressions that you can use wherever you go. These expressions are as easy as ABC This book will make you see English in a different light. Come and ride shotgun with us as we explore the wonders of idiomatic expressions.

We hope you'll enjoy this book.

Thank you!

The My English Routine Team

A)

A baker's dozen

Meaning: Not twelve but thirteen

Origin: This expression originated in 13th century England where many bakers were selling underweight loaves. Because of this, strict regulations were implemented on the proper weight of the loaves. Because of the old weighing system, bakers would add an extra loaf just to get the right weight of the loaves.

Example: She gave me a baker's dozen of donuts for the party.

A battle ax

Meaning: An overbearing and belligerent (usually middle-aged or old) woman

Origin: During the early years of the women's rights movements, a journal called "The Battle Axe" was published to help women to express their opinion on the change. Over the years, this expression was used to describe aggressive and domineering women of a certain age.

Example: Dahlia was the battle ax of the current situation.

A bitter pill to swallow

Meaning: A difficult experience to accept

Origin: It was inspired by medicines with bitter and horrid tastes. It was used figuratively in one citation from The Leavenworth Medical Herald, Volume 4 page 26, June 1870, and refers to changes made as a result of the Civil War:"

Example: Her new situation is a bitter pill to swallow.

A blessing in disguise

Meaning: A good thing that seemed bad at first

Origin: This idiom first originated during the mid-1700s. It first appeared in the 1746 poem "Reflections on a Flower-Garden" by English poet James Hervey.

Example: His entrance was a blessing in disguise.

A blue-eyed boy

Meaning: A favorite, a protege

Origin: This expression was taken from the image of a blue-eyed boy with fair hair which is often connected to innocence and chastity.

Example: He was that blue-eyed boy that my professor would always talk about.

A bunch of fives

Meaning: Punching someone

Origin: This expression was first used by Charles Westmacott in his book "The English Spy" in 1825. However, a lot of people believe that it was used"earlier in a book called "Boxiana" by Piece Egan. However, because both books are no longer available, they were not able to prove who was the first person to write this phrase. However, there is no doubt that this book is related to boxing.

Example: Koda was sent to detention after landing a bunch of fives.

A busman's holiday

Meaning: Spending one's holiday doing the same thing one would be doing at work

Origin: This idiom was taken from common practice for many horse-driven bus drivers in the past. Bus drivers who happened to be on holiday would often ride the bus that they usually drive just so they can check on the relief driver and how the horses are faring.

Example: Mikey is spending his day off like a busman's holiday.

A chip off the old block

Meaning: Children inherit certain traits from their parents.

Origin: This expression has several variations. It was first used in 1621 by Long Bishop Robert Sanderson's sermon referring to churchgoers as a son of Adam.

Example: Patrick is a chip off the old block. He looks very much like his father.

A couch potato

Meaning: Someone living life with minimum effort

Origin: A couch potato is often referred to as someone who is an inactive TV addict.

Example: A couch potato likes nothing but to laze around all day long.

A dead letter

Meaning: A law or practice is no longer observed.

Origin: This expression referred to the epistle of St. Paul comparing the life-giving spirit in the New Testament. In this case, most of the Mosaic Laws were no longer practiced by people in the New Testament.

Example: Child marriages are now a dead letter in the current society.

A dime a dozen

Meaning: Very common and of no particular value.

Origin: A dime is a small US coin worth ten cents which occurs in various US expressions as a metaphor for cheapness or smallness.

Example: Sierra thinks that she is just a dime a dozen singer.

A dish fit for the gods

Meaning: A very scrumptious or delectable meal

Origin: This expression was first coined by Shakespeare in his play titled Julius Caesar.

Example: Her carbonara is a dish fit for the gods.

A faint heart

Meaning: Heart timidity or lack of willpower prevents you from achieving your objective.

Origin: This expression is taken from the proverb "Faint heart never won fair lady" in the early 17th Century. However, this expression is said to have been coined two centuries earlier.

Example: Your faint heart will never let you succeed.

A feather in your cap

Meaning: An achievement to be proud of.

Origin: This expression used to be a sign of foolishness in the late 17th century. However, its meaning changed towards the mid-18th century.

Example: Your diploma will be the feather in your cap.

A finger in the/every pie

Meaning: To play a part in doing something; to interfere in a matter

Origin: This expression stems from the idea of a person trying to put his finger on every pie that he sees. This was then interpreted that this person is someone who meddles in certain things.

Example: Stop putting your finger in every pie! You are creating havoc with the people you are involved with.

A firm hand

Meaning: Strict discipline or control.

Origin: This expression was taken from the proverb "a firm hand on the reins (or the tiller)" It was inspired by the image of controlling a horse or a boat.

Example: Grandparents often tell parents to have a firm hand on their children.

A fish out of water

Meaning: Uncomfortable and restless, confused.

Origin: The idiom was taken from the allusion of getting fish out of the water. Getting the fish out of the water is a new and uncomfortable situation and kills it if it's removed from its habitat for a long time.

Example: She looks like a fish out of water in the crowd.

A fly on the wall

Meaning: Someone with the ability to observe a situation without anyone knowing

Origin: This expression was dated back to the early 20th century in the US. It was then used in a printed reference from the Oakland Tribune

(California) in February 1921. It says "I'd just love to be a fly on the wall when the Right Man comes along."

Example: Be careful about how you react to issues, there are tons of flies on the wall in this office.

A forlorn hope

Meaning: A faint remaining hope or chance; a desperate attempt.

Origin: In the mid-16th century, this expression was taken from the Dutch expression "verloren hoop" or "lost troop."

Example: With all my forlorn hope, I wish that everything would end up well given the current circumstance.

A glutton for punishment

Meaning: Continues to take the task that most people would avoid

Origin: This expression was inspired by the idea of gluttony or overeating without thinking of the possible abuses it can cause to your body.

Example: Mara is a glutton for punishment. She keeps saying yes to people's favors.

A golden age

Meaning: A period in the past when things were at their best, happiest, or most successful.

Origin: Taken from Greek and Roman Mythology, this expression was coined with the idea that the Golden Age was the happiest time of men's life. They believe that this was an era where they were able to succeed, and leave the barbaric and miserable ways of the Silver, Brass, and Iron ages.

Example: He loves reminiscing back to the times of his golden age.

A golden calf

Meaning: Something, especially wealth, as an object of excessive or unworthy worship.

Origin: This Biblical idiom was taken from the story of Moses in the Book of Exodus. In this story, the golden calf was a statue that many of the paganistic Israelites considered as one of their gods.

Example: I will make you a gold calf, to worship and take care of.

A good/bad/lucky break

Meaning: A good/bad opportunity, chance

Origin: This expression was originally taken from a game of pool. As the game starts, players try to break the positions of the clustered balls on the pool table with a cue ball. We call that a break. A good break happens when some of the balls get into the pockets while bad breaks are when the balls are situated in the most challenging positions.

Example: This lucky break paved her way to stardom in the showbiz industry.

A grain of mustard seed

Meaning: A small thing capable of vast development.

Origin: This is inspired by the idea of how a small black mustard seed grows into a large plant.

Example: Cryptocurrency is like a grain of mustard seed. It used to be small but look at how far it has made it.

A halfway house

Meaning: A compromise; the halfway point in a progression.

Origin: Half-way house used to be a place where many ex-prisoners or mental patients can stay to help get them reaccustomed to life outside prison. In the 18th century, the definition of the halfway house was changed into an inn located at the midpoint of two destinations. Travelers can stay in the halfway house before they resume their travel.

Example: We decided to stop at a halfway house instead of traveling the whole way.

A hatchet job

Meaning: To kill or discredit someone in the position.

Origin: The origin of this phrase started during US gang warfare. Large-scale Chinese gangs would often hire assassins to hack prominent people in rival gangs. Oftentimes, they hire hatchet men to do these jobs. Hatchet men would hack their victims with a hatchet.

Example: They did a hatchet job to stop him from getting sole authority.

A hostage to fortune

Meaning: An act, commitment, or remark which is regarded as unwise because it invites trouble or could prove difficult to live up to.

Origin: This expression was taken from an allusion to Francis Bacon's essay on marriage where he wrote 'He that hath wife and children hath given hostages to fortune.

Example: A lot of people consider marriage as something of a hostage of fortune.

A Judas kiss

Meaning: An act of betrayal, especially one disguised as a gesture of friendship

Origin: This expression is similar to the expression "kiss of death." This expression was taken from the betrayal of Judas Iscariot who had sold Jesus for 30 pieces of silver. It was cited in the book of Matthew 26:48 stating 'Whomsoever I shall kiss, that same is he: hold him fast.'

Example: She gave me a Judas kiss when she stole my role from me.

A leap in the dark

Meaning: A step of faith, a venture whose outcome cannot be predicted

Origin: It was first coined by Thomas Hobbes' last words before his death. He wrote, "Now I am about to take my last voyage, a great leap in the dark." Since then, this expression has been used by many philosophers in their writing.

Example: He took a leap in the dark despite not knowing what would happen tomorrow.

A little bird told me

Meaning: A secret source told me

Origin: This expression was said to come from Ecclesiastes 10:20 where it was written as 'Curse, not the King, no not in thy thought; and curse not the rich in thy bed-chamber: for a bird of the air shall carry the voice, and that which hath wings shall tell the matter.' Another possible theory would be the usage of birds as messengers back in the olden days.

Example: A little bird told me that you failed another exam today.

A lot on my plate

Meaning: Overwhelming task; too many tasks to do at the same time.

Origin: Originally, this expression was first used in the 1990s. The idea behind this expression talks about the amount of food that you have on your plate. It was then used figuratively.

Example: I'm going to pass on this outing. There is a lot on my plate right now.

A man's man

Meaning: A man whose personality is such that he is more popular and at ease with other men than with women.

Origin: This expression was first used in the story, "The Martian" by George Du Maurier. The phrase was defined as 'a good comrade par excellence, a frolicsome chum, a rollicking boon-companion, a jolly pal'.

Example: As handsome as he is, he is a man's man.

A movable feast

Meaning: A feast or an event that takes place at no regular time.

Origin: This expression was taken from contexts on the movable feast in the Christian Calendar. One of the examples of this feast is Easter Day. These celebrations are often celebrated on a specific day of the week but on different dates.

Example: Do we have a moveable feast this month to look forward to?

A nest egg

Meaning: Part of one's savings put aside as a reserve for the future

Origin: This expression was derived from chicken farming. To encourage their hens to lay more eggs, farmers would use a fake porcelain egg.

Example: Mina decided to put away a nest egg for her future investments.

A nine days wonder

Meaning: Something which aroused great interest that quickly fades

Origin: It was first cited by George Chaucer. He wrote 'A wonder lasts but nyne night never into une.' Etymologists believed that this expression was taken from the 9-day novenas of Catholicism.

Example: This book will be a nine days wonder for Sophie.

A pain in the neck

Meaning: An annoying or tedious person or thing

Origin: There is a clear origin of this expression. However, it comes from different vulgar variations that have been used from one country to another.

Example: This old couch is a pain in the neck.

A parting shot

Meaning: A final, pithy, or wounding remark, to which the listener has no chance of replying

Origin: Derived from a war tactic called Parthian shot. This strategy is used by skilled archers who fake retreat but turn around and fire their arrows with deadly accuracy.

Example: She left a parting shot before she left the room.

A pig in a poke

Meaning: A purchase that was not properly examined before it was made

Origin: Taken from old country fair customs, traders would often sell suckling piglets. Traders would show one piglet as proof while the rest are placed in pokes or sacks. Dishonest traders would often show a pig but put cats inside the pokes or sacks.

Example: Her new necklace is a pig in a poke.

A rough diamond

Meaning: Person with great qualities but with uncouth manners.

Origin: Literally, a rough diamond is a diamond before it has been cut and polished. A North American variant of this expression is a diamond in the rough.

Example: Jin was a rough diamond. It took them years to polish his skills.

A sight for sore eyes

Meaning: Happy to see the person.

Origin: This idiom dates back to the early 1700's During this era, this expression was used to denote something negative and opposite of the current meaning of this idiom. In recent years, this expression is used to denote something positive.

Example: Amira is a sight for sore eyes. I am very happy to see her.

A snail's pace

Meaning: Very slow movements or slow pace

Origin: This expression was used dating back to Middle English. During this era, snails are considered the epitome of slowness.

Example: The cars are moving at a snail's pace.

A square deal

Meaning: A fair bargain or treatment.

Origin: In the past, the word "square" was associated with the word 'honest". This expression was often used in a game of cards.

Example: All Sarah wanted was a square deal.

A stalking horse

Meaning: A less acceptable purpose hidden behind a more attractive facade.

Origin: This expression derived from a certain situation in the Middle Ages where marksmen would often find in getting a good shot. They would use a stalking horse to cover their marks from fowlers while stealthily hiding beneath the quarry.

Example: Her business looks like a stalking horse to me.

A stone's throw away

Meaning: Very close

Origin: There was no clear origin of this expression. However, it was a popular expression in 1830. It appeared in many printed references like the Three Course and a Desert by William Clarke and George Cruikshank. They wrote, "If you lived but a stone's throw away, I'd be wrong if I'd let you stir."

Example: Do not worry. I am a stone's throw away.

A straw poll

Meaning: A superficial test of opinion

Origin: This expression was first used in American Elections in the 1820s. The custom was to throw straws up in the air to determine the direction of the wind.

Example: I have done a straw poll on the current events happening right now.

A tangled web

Meaning: A complex, difficult, and confusing situation or thing.

Origin: This phrase was taken from Sir Walter Scott's epic poem Marmion (1808) where it was written as 'O what a tangled web we weave When first we practice to deceive!'

Example: This code is a tangled web! I can't seem to decode it.

A voice in the wilderness

Meaning: An unheeded advocate of reform.

Origin: This expression was taken from John the Baptist who proclaimed the coming of the Messiah.

Example: A voice in the wilderness says that she has to stop her ways to find happiness in herself.

A wet blanket

Meaning: Someone who has a depressing or discouraging effect on others.

Origin: This idiomatic expression was likened to the image of a wet blanket turning off the fire. Figuratively, the wet blanket refers to a gloomy person who can turn off the mood.

Example: Tina, don't be a wet blanket! It's a great day to be out in the sun.

A viper in your bosom

Meaning: A person you have helped but who behaves treacherously towards you.

Origin: Taken from the Aesop's Fable where a viper had bitten the bosom of its caretaker.

Example: Athy thought that Alpheus was the viper in Jenette's bosom.

Abandon ship

Meaning: To leave a dangerous situation

Origin: "Abandon ship" is an official command that is given by the captain when the ship is sinking.

Example: Fire! Everyone, Abandon ship! Please move towards the emergency exit.

Achilles' heel

Meaning: A weak or vulnerable spot in something or someone which is otherwise strong

Origin: This phrase originated from Greek Mythology. Thetis, the mother of Achilles, wanted to make her son invulnerable. So, she dipped him into the River Styx. Unfortunately, she was not able to dip Achilles's heel. His heel became his weak spot. Achilles was a strong and invincible warrior until Paris, the Prince of Troy shot him with an arrow in his heel.

Example: My grandma's Achilles' heel is her weak knees.

Across the board

Meaning: Applying to all.

Origin: The origin of this idiom refers to the horse-racing bet in which the equal amounts of the stakes on the horse are the same amount regardless if you win or lose.

Example: The laws against discrimination were made across the board. Everyone should be treated kindly despite their color, gender, or socioeconomic status.

Act of God

Meaning: An instance of uncontrollable natural forces in operation.

Origin: This idiom refers to the natural calamities that often happen. It is said to be an act of God and not influenced by men.

Example: The tsunami was an act of God that no one can ever defy.

Add another string to your bow

Meaning: To add more than one skill or opportunity.

Origin: This expression came from archery. During Medieval times, bows and arrows were the main weapons used in hunting and long-distance defense. Because of this, a competition between men came to be. The person who had the best bow was the winner. To secure their victory, archers attached another string to their bow. This way, in case the first string broke in the first round, they had a backup string to continue their competition. That's how the expression came to be

Example: We need to add another string to your bow to ensure that you will get better opportunities in the future.

Against all odds

Meaning: To be able to succeed despite the adversaries.

Origin: Originally the title of the book by F.W Currey. It was constantly used as a positive affirmation idiom/expression in many books, songs, and movies.

Example: I was able to make it through college against all odds.

Against the clock

Meaning: Running out of time

Origin: This expression dates back to the 1900s. It sprung from sports that individually timed participants as the fastest among the group.

Example: Michael is fighting against the clock. He has not finished his schoolwork yet.

Against the grain

Meaning: Contrary to the natural inclination or feeling of someone or something.

Origin: This expression was taken from the idea that wood is much easier to cut when you cut with the grain, instead of against the grain.

Example: I had to go against the grain after my parents said that they want me to become a lawyer.

Ahead of the curve

Meaning: Equipped with the best features. Ahead of the current trends.

Origin: This expression was taken from the US military during the 1970s. It was first used by President Nixon when talking to his inner circles when giving information to the public before it became common knowledge.

Example: Apple Inc always strives to be ahead of the curve in terms of technology.

Alive and kicking

Meaning: Very active, lively

Origin: This expression is a food idiom that refers to the newly caught fish in the market. The fish vendor used to say "alive and kicking" to refer to the fact that the fish is fresh from the ocean.

Example: After being confined in the hospital for a week, I am back alive and kicking.

All at sea

Meaning: Feeling lost or confused.

Origin: Originated in the early era of exploration. If a person is "at sea", they are more likely lost in the sea with no assurance of coming back.

Example: I am all at sea because of what happened to them.

All hands on deck

Meaning: An activity

Origin: This naval idiom was used when the captain requires the attention of everyone in the crew or when there are certain things that need to be discussed with everybody in the ship.

Example: All hands on deck, everybody! We have a new project.

All in the same boat

Meaning: The same situation

Origin: First used during the time of Ancient Greece when people were constantly going to war. People of different statuses were all riding the same boat to war.

Example: The pandemic has taught us that we are all in the same boat.

All roads lead to Rome

Meaning: There are many different ways of reaching the same goal or conclusion.

Origin: This old idiom was based on the fact that Rome used to be the point of convergence in all the roads in the Roman Empire. This idiom can be compared to the medieval Latin phrase "mille vie ducunt hominem per secula Romam", meaning 'a thousand roads lead a man forever towards Rome'.

Example: Do not give up on your goal, remember all roads lead to Rome.

All sewn up

Meaning: All done and completed.

Origin: Because of the lack of coffins and burial grounds on the sea, sailors would sew their dead comrades inside a hammock and roll it into the sea. They would attach a heavy object on it to weigh it down.

Example: Now that it's all sewn up, we are ready to start another task.

All the buzz

Meaning: Something exciting

Origin: Started during the late 20th century when people were likening buzz with excitement and trend. This expression is still used even now.

Example: With all the buzz that's happening, I am looking forward to the next season of this TV series.

All's fair in love and war

Meaning: A situation where standard rules do not apply

Origin: This expression was created by Renaissance English poet and playwright John Lyly's popular book, Euphues the Anatomy of Wit (1578). The actual quote was, "The rules of fair play do not apply in love and war."

Example: All is fair in love and war; it goes the same with football.

An admirable Crichton

Meaning: Person who excels in all kinds of studies and pursuits, or who is noted for supreme competence.

Origin: This idiom referred to James Crichton of Clunie. Crichton was a renowned nobleman because of his intelligence and physical strength. In the play by J.M Barrie, Crichton was the hero who took charge of the manor when his master's family was shipwrecked on a deserted island.

Example: Celeste is indeed an admirable Crichton.

An arm and a leg

Meaning: The cost of sacrifice; Very expensive

Origin: The origin of this expression started after the American Civil War. Due to the injuries sustained by the soldiers, Congress had enacted a special pension for these war veterans.

Example: It cost me an arm and a leg to get this limited edition bag.

An eager beaver

Meaning: An overly zealous person, one who tries to impress others with enthusiasm and hard work

Origin: This expression stemmed from the idea of how hard-working beavers are. Its enthusiasm is considered as being eager.

Example: Anna is an eager beaver, it sometimes puts her in the wrong spot.

An even break

Meaning: A fair chance.

Origin: This expression was popularized from W. C. Fields' catchphrase 'Never give a sucker an even break'. It was first used in a 1923 musical called Poppy.

Example: I'm going to give you an even break, make sure you give your best shot.

An honest broker

Meaning: A disinterested intermediary or mediator.

Origin: This expression was taken from the German phrase "ehrlicher makler". In 1878 it was then used by German Statesman Bismarck in his speech about his recommendation of adopting this role in peacemaking.

Example: We need an honest broker to be our judge for this case.

An iron curtain

Meaning: An impenetrable barrier, especially the Iron Curtain, the physical and other barriers preventing the passage of people and information

Origin: In the 18th century, the Iron curtain in the theater was used to refer to a fire curtain. However, during World War II. The "iron curtain" became a wall that stopped people and information from going in and out of the Soviet Bloc.

Example: She had placed herself in an iron curtain

An old chestnut

Meaning: A tired old joke; any overly familiar topic

Origin: This expression was originally taken from an English Melodrama where the American actor William Warren quoted one of the quotes from the play called the Broken Sword. He said 'A chestnut. I should know as well as you, having heard you tell the tale twenty-seven times, and I'm sure it was a chestnut.'

Example: Stop telling that joke! I have been hearing about that old chestnut for a long time.

An old wives' tale

Meaning: Superstitious belief.

Origin: This expression dates back to the early 16th century when it was cited in Tyndale's translation of the Bible.

Example: There are many old wives tales in the world that have interesting stories behind them.

An ugly duckling

Meaning: A young person who turns out to be beautiful or talented against all expectations.

Origin: This expression was taken from the fairy tale by Hans Christian Andersen with the same title. It talks about how an 'ugly duckling' that was mocked and isolated became a beautiful swan.

Example: Chloe used to be an ugly duckling. But now, she has grown into a beautiful swan.

And all that jazz

Meaning: And such similar things.

Origin: In the past, jazz was referred to as "meaningless talk" despite being used in a musical sense. This expression developed to its current meaning during the mid-20th century.

Example: Just cleaning my room and all that jazz.

Another day, another dollar...

Meaning: Being paid for what you are doing

Origin: This American Naval expression was often used in the literal sense. This expression originated during the 19th century. Sailors were paid $1 per day.

Example: Another day, another dollar; we all went home after a busy day at work.

Apple of discord

Meaning: Something which causes strife, argument, rivalry

Origin: Apple of discord is an expression inspired by the story of Helen of Troy. This apple was a revenge by Eris, the goddess of Discord, who was not invited to the wedding of Thetis and Peleus. She threw a golden apple bearing the words "for the most beautiful". This led to an all out war between the cities in Greece.

Example: Her words were the apple of discord that caused their current predicament.

Apple of my eye

Meaning: Loved by everyone

Origin: This expression first appeared in the year 885. It was written in Alfred the Great's Anglo-Saxon version of the book "Pastoral Care" by Pope Gregory I. This book was written to teach clergymen how to perform their pastoral duties. This phrase was then used in Shakespeare's A Midsummer Night's Dream in 1605. In the play, the fairy Robin Goodfellow acquires a flower once hit by Cupid's arrow. He dropped some of the juice of the flower into a sleeping man's eyes while uttering the words, "Flower of this purple dye, Hit with Cupid's archery, sank in the apple of his eye."

Example: My daughter is the apple of my eye.

Apple-pie bed

Meaning: A practical joke in which a bed is made using only one sheet, folded over partway down the bed, thus preventing the would-be occupant from stretching out.

Origin: This expression was taken from the French nappe plie (folded cloth). However, this expression was also referring to apple turnover, a folded pastry with a sweet apple filling in the middle.

Example: She made an apple-pie bed for her daughter to keep her moving too much throughout the night.

Armed to the teeth

Meaning: Overly equipped with something

Origins: Originated during the 17th century when pirates were over-armed with guns and a knife in between their teeth.

Example: Parents have armed their kids to the teeth. You will never know what your kids would need in summer camp.

As cool as a cucumber

Meaning: Someone who can face any kind of situation

Origin: It was originally from a song by John Gay. He likened himself to a cucumber that is calm, cool, and collected.

Example: Jamie is a person who is as cool as a cucumber.

As easy (or simple) as ABC

Meaning: Extremely easy or straightforward.

Origin: This expression referred to the child's first educational lesson which is the ABCs

Example: If only Math is as easy as ABC, many of us would have passed Trigonometry.

As fresh as a daisy

Meaning: Alert and full of energy

Origin: Daisies were said to be flowers that never get tired because they close at night and open up during the day.

Example: After taking a long nap, Sean looks as fresh as a daisy.

As happy as a clam

Meaning: Happy and content

Origin: It refers to clams' behavior during the high tide. Other predators tend to swim away during the high tide but clams are swimming and frolicking happily during the high tide.

Example: The baby is as happy as a clam when she is full and clean.

As happy as a lark

Meaning: Happy and cheerful

Origin: This expression is likened to a lark, which is a type of songbird that loves to create cheerful songs."

Example: Children are happy as a lark whenever they go to the playground.

As plain as a pikestaff

Meaning: Totally obvious, evident; easy to understand

Origin: This expression was derived from a pikestaff that is often used in the infantry. The pike is similar to a spear but with a long visible shaft to many people. Although there are several theories of this expression, the modern theory is probably the closest to its actual meaning.

Example: Her dress looks as plain as a pikestaff.

As sick as a parrot

Meaning: Extremely disappointed

Origin: Originated during the 1970s, this expression was probably inspired by the disease called psittacosis or parrot fever. This disease can be transferred from the sick cage bird to men.

Example: I was as sick as a parrot to learn the news that I didn't win first prize.

As the crow flies

Meaning: In a straight line; the shortest distance between two points

Origin: During the early era of exploration, navigational tools were very limited. However, this did not stop English explorers in their search for land. They carried a huge cage of crows. Crows are known to be intelligent birds that would fly off in search of a food source. The crows were released on top of the mast. The captain followed the path of the crow which led them to the nearby island in the shortest time.

Examples: He was moving as the crow flew.

At a loose end

Meaning: Idle, with no plans and nothing to do

Origin: This expression comes from the tall sailing ships. They often have tons of rope that help hold the sails in place." But because of the strong winds that move the sails, the ropes become loose and sometimes they unravel. Thus, it was a sailor's job to tend to these ropes 24/7. This was to keep the ropes from getting loose while the ship was sailing. If the captain saw sailors being idle, he would make them do the ropes for the whole day.

Example: Lara left everything at a loose end.

At cross purposes

Meaning: With aims or goals that conflict or interfere with one another.

Origin: This expression traces back to the 17th century when it was taken from the game called "cross-purpose" or "cross-questions". In this game, people are given a series of questions where they have to give ridiculous answers to another question.

Example: They are at cross purposes; we need to find a way how we can merge our goals together without clashing with each other.

At daggers drawn

Meaning: In a state of bitter enmity.

Origin: This expression was taken from the idea of drawing daggers before the actual fight happens. This expression was first cited in 1668. It has been used since then.

Example: Last night, you look like your daggers were drawn.

At half cock

Meaning: When only partly ready.

Origin: This expression was taken from gun usage. Half-cock happens when the cock of the gun is lifted but not moved to a position that will trigger the gun to shoot.

Example: Dana was packing at half cock before I arrived.

At odds

Meaning: In disagreement

Origin: The origin of this expression remains unknown. However, many people believe in the concept of odd and even. They used to refer to odd as something that both parties would differ. This expression was coined in the 1300s.

Example: Mila and her brother are currently at odds on their opinions about the current events in the country.

At sixes and sevens

Meaning: Talks about disagreement between two people.

Origin: This idiom originates back in the 14th century. It was traced back during the disputes of the Merchant Taylors (tailors) and the Skin Livery Companies (fur makers). Their arguments center on the Order of Precedence where they argue who should be in the sixth place. The argument was solved by Sir Robert Billesden who swapped the two groups at the feast of Corpus Christi. Since then, these two groups alternate between the sixth and seventh place in the Order of Precedence every year.

Example: Mila and Yuri are often at sixes and sevens with each other.

At the drop of a hat

Meaning: Immediately, without hesitation or need for persuasion

Origin: During the days of the American frontier, it was a custom to drop a hat to signal competitors that the bout is starting.

Example: At the drop of a hat, she had let go of his hand.

At the end of one's rope

Meaning: Running out of patience

Origin: This expression was inspired by animals that are tethered or staked out on the farm. When you say at the end of the rope then it would mean that you have reached the maximum distance between you and the tether.

Example: She was at the end of her rope after seeing the mess that they had made.

At the end of the day

Meaning: Tried and true

Origin: This modern idiom is often used in literary forms to signify a certain fact that will not change the situation.

Example: At the end of the day, you will always have your family with you.

At the end of your tether

Meaning: Having no patience, resources, or energy left to cope with something.

Origin: This expression is similar to the expression "to the end of one's rope". It refers to an image of grazing at the end of the rope or tether.

Example: The teacher is at the end of her tether about how rowdy her students are getting.

At the helm

Meaning: In command or in-charge

Origin: This expression stems from the helm, which is the steering mechanism of the boat. If you are at the helm, it means to say that you are the person in charge of navigating the boat.

Example: He is at the helm of all this craziness.

Baby blues

Meaning: Postpartum depression; blue eyes

Origin: This idiom came to be during World War II. During that time, it used to refer to babies born with blue eyes. This was due to the lack of melanin pigmentation in the children. It was only in the year 1940 that it was used to refer to mothers falling to depression after childbirth.

Example: My mother had baby blues after my sister Charlie was born.

Backroom boys

Meaning: Researchers, scientists, etc., whose hard work is essential but is not brought to public attention

Origin: This expression was first coined by Lord Beaverbrook in his speech for the unsung heroes during the war on March 24, 1941: 'To whom must praise be given? I will tell you. It is the boys in the backroom. They do not sit in the limelight but they are the men who do the work.'

Example: The backroom boys were able to create one of the best inventions in the world.

Badger to death

Meaning: To harass or persecute someone.

Origin: Originated from the practice called badger-baiting which pits a badger against a dog.

Example: Many people have been badgered to death in foreign countries because of their nationalities.

Ball and chain

Meaning: Something that keeps you from doing what you want.

Origin: This device was used to restrain prisoners from the 17th to the 20th century. However, in the current context, this refers to wives who keep a close watch on their husbands.

Example: He was balled and chained to his work.

Bang for the buck

Meaning: More value for money: a good deal.

Origin: This expression comes from a political origin. The word "bang" often refers to bombs and weapons while buck means money. This expression was first recorded in 1954 by US Defense Secretary Charles Erwin Wilson who used this expression as the title of the New Look policy of depending on nuclear weapons. His speech aimed to rely more on nuclear arms instead of the regular army.

Example: Dan promised his mother more bang for the buck.

Bare bones

Meaning: Basic or essential facts of something

Origin: This expression was likened to an idea of a skinny person where you can already see the bone structure of the person. This idiom was first cited in 1598 and gained its popularity after the 1940s.

Example: The teacher just gave us the bare bones of our research.

Barefaced liar

Meaning: Someone who lies with no shame

Origin: This expression was first used in Harriet Beecher Stowe's classic novel titled Uncle Tom's Cabin,

Example: She is a barefaced liar. She makes everything sound so true.

Barging in

Meaning: To interrupt or disturb

Origin: The word barge refers to a vessel with a flat bottom that is difficult to maneuver at the sea. They often need large momentum to move and stop.

Example: If you notice, pets are known for barging in on crucial meetings.

Barking dogs seldom bite

Meaning: Appear fierce or scary, but to be weak in reality

Origin: This expression was taken to an allusion from a dog who is busy barking but doesn't bite at all.

This old English proverb alludes to a dog that is busy barking, but can't bite. It's not talking about dogs in reality but as a metaphor for someone who speaks a lot but doesn't follow through with actions.

Example: Barking dogs seldom bite, that's just who he is.

Barking up the wrong tree

Meaning: Following a false lead or having misguided thoughts about a situation or event.

Origin: This idiom first came about when hunting dogs bark up at their prey that are in the trees. But sometimes, these dogs are not able to see that their prey has already escaped. They continue to bark up the wrong tree.

Example: He wouldn't stop barking up the wrong tree; Jed failed.

Batten down the hatches

Meaning: Prepare for trouble or hard times

Origin: This nautical idiom originated during the 1800s. Around this time, ships that were carrying cargo usually had hatchways. Hatches were often left open to allow ventilation in the ship. However, during rough seas, the captain would call to "batten down the hatches." This way, they can stop water from hitting the cargo or filling the boat. Hatches were often covered with tarpaulin to keep water from getting in.

Example: We learned our lesson from the supertyphoon. We should always batten down the hatches.

Be all fingers and thumbs

Meaning: Thumbs are clumsy or awkward in your actions.

Origin: This expression was taken from the idea in the mid-16th century where all the fingers in your hands were imagined as thumbs. The lack of dexterity of the thumb makes your actions clumsy.

Example: We could be all fingers and thumbs in awkward moments.

Be on the lookout

Meaning: Keep searching for someone or something that is wanted; be alert to danger or trouble.

Origin: The word "lookout" was originally taken from the naval and military context. However, in the 17th century, lookouts were sentries who were tasked to keep watch throughout the day and night.

Example: I want you to be on the lookout for the next cosmetic sale this month.

Be the death of

Meaning: Cause someone's death.

Origin: This expression comes from an unknown origin. However, it was often used as an exaggerated or funny way of dying from laughing, boredom, embarrassment, and other similar emotions.

Example: You will be the death of me.

Beat a dead horse

Meaning: To engage in a fruitless effort.

Origin: This expression is a mariner's term that refers to the" horse latitudes". The horse latitudes is an area where the winds were irregular and unreliable, about 30 degrees on either side of the equator. This area often had high pressure which resulted in weak winds and the sea was calm for a long period of time. Sailors were often paid in advance before the voyage. The time it took to pay the advance off was known as the dead horse. Because they were paid in advance, sailors saw little point in working on clearing the area. That's how the expression "beating the dead horse" came to be.

Example: They beat a dead horse on this project.

Beat around the bush

Meaning: To circle the point; to avoid the point

Origin: Originated as a hunting practice in Britain. For you to catch a game fowl, you need to beat the bushes.

Example: Stop beating around the bush and tell me what you have to say.

Beat me to the punch

Meaning: One upped; someone who was able to reach or do something before you

Origin: This boxing idiomatic expression was popularized in a song by Smokey Robinson and Ronald White entitled You Beat Me to the Punch which meant exactly the same as the expression.

Example: He had beat me to the punch in that race.

Beck and call

Meaning: To be available to someone whenever you need them to be.

Origin: This expression was taken from the word "beckon" in the 18th century. This word is used to call or signal someone to come over.

Example: I will be here at your beck and call.

Bee in your bonnet

Meaning: Fixated on something and can not think of anything else but it.

Origin: This expression was dated to the 18th century. This expression was inspired by the idea of bees buzzing inside one's bonnet.

Example: Sierra had a bee in her bonnet. She is currently obsessed with her favorite idol.

Bee's knees

Meaning: Excellence or perfection.

Origin: This expression came to be during the 1920s. It was then a certain part of the body with an animal. There were tons of variations that came to be. One of them is the bee's knees.

Example: This artwork is the bee's knees!

Beef up

Meaning: To build muscles or develop something; to become stronger

Origin: This refers to the idea of raising cattle breeds. In order to get a large quantity of meat, cattle owners would feed these cattle more to fatten them before slaughter.

Example: Evan wants to beef up and build his self-confidence.

Been there, done that

Meaning: Used to express past experience of or familiarity with something.

Origin: A 20th-century idiom that describes the boredom of doing things on a constant basis.

Example: Zip lines are not that great. Been there, done that. You should try bungee jumping instead.

Below the belt

Meaning: An unfair or underhanded tactic

Origin: This expression was originally from boxing. When the London Prize Ring Rules were drafted by a boxer named Jack Broughton, he had stated that no man should hit below the belt or waist. It was later added as a formal code by the Marquess of Queensberry in 1867. This expression continued to evolve throughout the years. It has been used inside the boxing ring and figuratively as well.

Example: How do you expect John to win when Rob was hitting below the belt?

Bend over backward

Meaning: To do anything to make the other person happy

Origin: It was originally a slogan for Cuna Supply Cooperative which said "When you need a loan, we bend over backward to help"

Example: A father will bend over backward just to see his daughter's smiling face.

Beneath your dignity

Meaning: Of too little importance or value for you to do it.

Origin: The Latin equivalent is "infra dignitatem", and the humorous abbreviation of this, "infra dig", is sometimes used in informal contexts.

Example: Spreading rumors is way beneath your dignity.

Beyond the veil

Meaning: In a mysterious or hidden place or state, especially the unknown state of existence after death.

Origin: Originally taken from the figurative veil that hid the innermost sanctuary of Jerusalem. Later on, people started referring to it as the mystical division between this world and another dimension.

Example: There are secrets that are yet to be uncovered beyond the veil.

Big cheese

Meaning: Influential person

Origin: This expression originated in 1802 when Thomas Jefferson received a 500 kg cheese. However, in the early 20th century slicing up a cake by a VIP was considered a special ceremony.

Example: Let's get a big cheese to help with our marketing campaign.

Big mouth

Meaning: Someone who talks too much; someone who shares secrets that are meant to be kept private

Origin: This expression was probably created in the late 1800s and early 1900s. It was a belief taken from Americanism and American culture.

Example: Please try not to open your big mouth and spill anything today.

Big shoes to fill

Meaning: The successor of a person who was a great individual and accomplished much will likely be judged accordingly.

Origin: First used by Andrew Jackson when he assumed the position of the President of the United States.

Example: As the new mayor of the town, Mr. Smith has big shoes to fill.

Birds of a feather flock together

Meaning: People with similar interests would like to find each other and keep each other company.

Origin: This expression was originally in a literary piece in which William Turner used a form of it in his 'papist satire' (writing against the Roman Catholic religion) The Rescuing of Romish Fox.

Example: If you are looking for Sara, make sure to look for Paul. After all, birds of a feather flock together.

Bite off more than you can chew

Meaning: You have taken on a project or task that is beyond what you are capable of.

Origins: This saying dates back to 1800s America when people often chewed tobacco. Sometimes the chewer would put into their mouth more than they could fit; it's quite self-explanatory!

Example: Stop! You are biting off more than you can chew.

Bite the bullet

Meaning: To endure something difficult or unpleasant.

Origin: Originated from the 1891 novel titled "The Light that Failed." In the book, "bite the bullet" used to be a practice where a patient would bite on a bullet to cope with the excruciating pain from surgery.

Example: She was in deep pain. She had to bite the bullet to endure the whole surgery.

Bite the dust

Meaning: To be finished, to be worn out; to die

Origin: This expression was originally meant to fall in battle. However, because of the several translations of Homer's Iliad, this expression was then used on almost anything that gets worn out or broken.

Example: They had no choice but to bite the dust after finishing last in the race.

Bitter end

Meaning: The absolute end; the last extremity

Origin: This nautical idiom talks about the post called bitts. During olden times, sailors would often tie their anchors to these bitts. Sailors would put color cloth before the rope had reached the bitt. So when the rope reached the bitt, it signified that the anchor could not go any further. They called this the bitter end. If the rope lets out a bitter end, it means to say that the rope has reached its maximum length or the water is too deep already.

Example: The drama ended up with a bitter end.

Black and blue

Meaning: Physically, emotionally or mentally bruised.

Origin: The idea behind this idiom was taken from the colors that bruises would make on your skin. The expression "black and blue" is more often associated with a person being beaten to death than of an accident.

Example: He was all black and blue after I saw her leave the principal's office.

Black hole

Meaning: An area where lost things can never be recovered: An area where communication is not viable.

Origin: A black hole is an area in Space where the gravity is strong and things can be sucked into it, including the light. People thought that a black hole was formed because of a collapsing star.

Example: This area is a black hole. I don't have a signal or anything.

Black sheep

Meaning: Refers to someone who is feared and disliked. Most of the time, it refers to someone in the family.

Origin: This expression was inspired by Bible where people were referred to as sheep and the Lord is the shepherd. At this time, black sheep were also considered less valuable and considered bad and evil.

Example: Nico is the black sheep in the family.

Blazing row

Meaning: Heated and angry argument

Origin: There is no known origin for this expression. However, the word row used to refer to "disagreement." Adding the word "blazing" would give you an idea that the argument didn't end well.

Example: We had a blazing row about certain things that we don't normally disagree on.

Blind leading blind

Meaning: Incompetent people advising or guiding others who are equally incapable

Origin: This expression comes with two different citations of its earlier use. One was taken from the Bible. Matthew 15:14 reads, "Let them alone: They be blind leaders of blind. And if the blind lead the blind, both shall fall into the ditch". It was also written in the Upanishads where it was written as "Abiding in the midst of ignorance, thinking themselves wise and learned, fools for aimlessly hither and thither, like blind led by the blind."

Example: Don't vote for the wrong person. It's like the blind leading blind.

Blind spot

Meaning: An area in which one fails to exercise judgment or discrimination; A portion of a field that cannot be seen or observed with existing equipment.

Origin: The word blind spot refers to the area of the map that is not blocked by certain features like mountains. Figuratively, it also refers to the lack of awareness of a person about a certain issue.

Example: Always be careful when driving in winding areas. There are a lot of blind spots.

Blood money

Meaning: Gaining something at the expense of someone

Origin: There are possible origins of this expression. Blood money can be the price paid to a hired killer. It can also be the price paid to recruiters for their questionable recruitment tactics or the reward that privateers get for capturing an enemy ship

Example: He was accused of accepting blood money from his clients.

Blood, sweat, and tears

Meaning: It means the huge amount of effort exerted on a certain circumstance.

Origin: Originally taken from the Sermons on Various Subjects by Christmas Evans (1766-1838), where Christ was bathed in his blood, sweat, and tears to save humanity

Example: After putting all the blood, sweat, and tears into this project, Sara can finally smile after seeing that the launch was a successful one.

Blow a fuse

Meaning: Lose your temper.

Origin: This expression is linked to an engine where it blows a gasket.

Example: He will blow a fuse when he learns that you broke his car.

Blow hot and cold

Meaning: Alternate inconsistently between two moods, attitudes, or courses of action; be sometimes enthusiastic, sometimes unenthusiastic about something.

Origin: This expression was taken from a fable where a traveler was offered hospitality by a satyr but offended him.

Example: Women on their periods often blow hot and cold.

Blow one's mind

Meaning: Something surreal: Something shocking

Origin: This expression was originally likened to the effects of LSD during the 1960s. However, in the later years, it was used to indicate something shocking or surreal.

Example: Serena's mind will be blown when she sees her surprise.

Blow one's own horn

Meaning: Means to boast about one's own achievements.

Origins: Though phrases meaning the same thing had been in use for centuries, the actual expression is first recorded by Anthony Trollope in his 1873 work titled Australia and New Zealand.

Example: Stop blowing your own horn when you haven't done anything significant.

Blowing smoke

Meaning: Making insincere or meaningless compliments

Origin: Originally inspired by magicians during magic shows when they awe people with magic. However, in later years, the meaning of the word evolved to making meaningless compliments to gain another person's trust.

Example: Stop blowing smoke if you don't mean anything from it.

Blue blood

Meaning: People that come from privileged, wealthy, or powerful families.

Origin: Referred to royals with blue-ish veins and pale skin. In Europe, blue blood can only happen if both parents are from pure royal families.

Example: She is one of the blue blood living on the wealthier side of time.

Bluestocking

Meaning: An erudite woman

Origin: This expression was taken from a society founded in 1400 in Venice called the Della Calza. Della Calza was literally translated as "of the stocking" and its emblem bore a bluestocking.

Example: This blue stocking keeps impressing me with her knowledge.

Bone to pick

Meaning: A lengthy discussion or argument

Origin: This expression dates back to the 16th century. It was often referred to as a dog, endlessly removing the meat in a huge bone.

Example: I have a bone to pick with Matthew.

Bones day

Meaning: A fruitful or productive day

Origin: This expression is a fairly new idiom. This expression was coined in 2021 by Jonathan Graziano in his Tik Tok account. "Bones or no Bones day" was inspired by his 13-year-old Pug named Noodles.

If Noodles flop on the floor, it means that you won't be doing anything at all. But if he doesn't, then you need to do something productive.

Example: Today is going to be a bones day, regardless of what Noodles would say.

Born with a silver spoon in one's mouth

Meaning: Someone who inherited wealth; a spoiled person who comes from a rich family

Origin: It was inspired by the 1840 book "Gold Spoon Oration" which criticized President Martin Van Buren for his luxurious lifestyle.

Example: Sebastian is someone born with a silver spoon in his mouth. But yet he remains humble.

Bottom line

Meaning: Net income, final figure on a profit

Origin: This accounting idiom was first used during the 1970s. It was first used during the economic decline of a Kansas City marketing firm.

Example: The bottom line of this week's profit is finally increasing.

Bottoms up!

Meaning: Express friendly feelings towards one's companions before drinking.

Origin: During the 18th and 19th centuries, many English Navy recruiters would coerce many drinkers to join the service. They would venture to the dockside pubs to recruit unsuspecting drinkers. During this time, a "King's Shilling" was proof that an agreement had been made between the recruiter and the recruitee. However, some recruiters would deceive recruits by dropping a shilling into their quarts. This unknowing victim would only realize what happened after they found themselves in the middle of the sea.

Example: It was a successful business venture! Bottom's up, everyone!

Brain drain

Meaning: The migration of highly skilled or trained people from a particular country

Origin: This expression was first coined by the Royal Society about the emigration of many scientists and engineers to North America after the post war events in Europe. Hence, "brain drain" because of the lack of scientists and engineers in Europe.

Example: The country has suffered a brain drain from the doctors leaving for greener pastures.

Break a leg

Meaning: It means good luck

Origin: This expression was first used in the German theater with the expression

Hals- und Beinbruch which means "a broken neck and a broken leg." However, it uses reverse psychology.

Example: Do well on your exams! Break a leg!

Break open

Meaning: Open something or someone with the use of force.

Origin: This phrase comes from a Biblical account of Paul and Silas. They were praying in their prison cell when a big quake came and broke the prison doors.

Example: We used the nutcracker to break open the crab's hard shell.

Break the ice

Meaning: To end conflict or initiate friendship.

Origin: The phrase came from the 1580s when trading countries would break the ice for their trading ship for them to pass.

Example: Sierra had to break the ice for everyone in the room.

Break the mold

Meaning: Do something different than what is expected from you.

Origin: This expression is taken from pottery where they used to cast artifacts in molds. If one breaks the mold, the artifact can not be copied by others." will not be copied by others.

Example: He decided to break the mold and become a writer instead of being a doctor or a lawyer like his parents.

Break the news

Meaning: To make something known to everybody; Inform everyone of the most important news.

Origin: This expression dated back to the Medieval era. During this time, medieval messengers would carry a rolled sealed parchment. Once the messenger broke the seal, the news was revealed to the recipient.

Example: I hate to be the one to break the news but we have a test today.

Breath of fresh air

Meaning: A sense of welcome relief

Origin: This idiomatic expression was first used in an article of the Electric Magazine of Foreign Literature, Science and Art in May 1845. They likened it to something which changed the course of the situation.

Example: Her smile is a breath of fresh air.

Bring out the 'A' game

Meaning: Do your best

Origin: First used in the early 1990s to cheer the Chicago Bulls. This expression has been a favorite of many coaches and reporters.

Example: Let's bring out our "A" game on the championship leg!

Brown study

Meaning: Melancholy mood accompanied by deep thought

Origin: In Old English, colors are often used to convey a person's emotions. Brown is often referred to as being sad and lonely. It was first cited in the book called Dice-Play where it was written as "Lack of company will soon lead a man into a brown study."

Example: I am stuck in brown study while everybody is out doing their thing.

Brownie points

Meaning: Imaginary extra credit for doing something for someone.

Origin: There are several origins for the expression "brownie points." One of them is the brown ration stamps that were used to buy food during World War II. George Brown, a railway superintendent, used this method to price his underlings.

Example: I am planning to get some brownie points on this project. I hope Ms. Rodriguez will be kind enough not to fail me in her subject.

Bucket list

Meaning: A list of achievement or experience in a person's lifetime; Things that they long to do.

Origin: The bucket list is closely related to the idiom "kick the bucket" When a person kicks the bucket, it also goes with the idea of list dying as well. Hence, before the person kicks the bucket, he wants to accomplish the things in his list.

Example: My bucket list is filled with things that I want to do.

Buffer zone

Meaning: Neutral zone between two or more areas

Origin: The origin of this expression is currently unknown. However, this expression is a popular military and political expression. It is often used to describe the neutral tract of land between the opposing forces.

Example: This area is the buffer zone, we are safe here.

Building blocks

Meaning: Basic step or part of something

Origin: This expression was taken from the idea of a toy called building blocks and creating a building. In order to build a good building, one must have a strong foundation to make it carry the weight of the building.

Example: Learning SEO is one of the building blocks that she has to learn.

Bun in the oven

Meaning: Pregnant.

Origin: This expression was originally from the novel Cruel Sea, a novel by Nicholas Monserrate. One of his characters named Bennet cited the expression "I bet you left a bun in the oven, both of you".

Example: My sister has a bun in the oven. I am officially going to be an aunt again.

Burn the midnight oil

Meaning: To work late into the night.

Origin: Before electricity was invented, people used oil to illuminate their houses. In the past, whale oil was considered one of the most expensive oils on the market. If you were to be working all night, then your projects must have been important because you burned all your expensive oil to complete them.

Example: She has to burn the midnight oil to cram for her exams.

Burning ears

Meaning: When someone is being talked about.

Origin: This idiom originated from an ancient Roman belief. It says that if you feel a burning or a tingling sensation in your ears, then someone is talking about you. If it's the left ear, it means that they are talking badly about you. If it's the right ear, then they are praising you.

Example: Someone is talking behind my back, I can feel my ears burning.

Burst one's bubble

Meaning: To destroy one's hopes and dream

Origin: This expression was associated with the word "gaining steam". It has been used in many literary works since then.

Example: I am sorry to burst your bubble, but all the tickets for this concert are sold out.

Bush telegraph

Meaning: A rapid informal spreading of information or rumor; the network through which this takes place.

Origin: This expression dates back to the 19th century. It referred to the group of people who are bushrangers who are looking for information.

Example: The information of her sudden marriage spread like a bush telegraph.

Bust one's balls

Meaning: To work hard or be punished.

Origin: This idiom referred to the practice of castrating a bull to a steer. In the past, the way to castrate a calf was to break its testicles.

Example: We need to bust our balls if we want to submit this before the deadline.

Butter someone up

Meaning: To praise or flatter someone excessively

Origin: Inspired by an Indian practice where they throw butterballs of ghee at the statues of their gods. They believe that by doing so, they can seek favor and forgiveness from their gods in the new year.

Example: He had to butter up his mother to avoid getting detention.

By and large

Meaning: On the whole; everything considered; in general

Origin: This idiom is a nautical term that originated from two idioms. The expression "by" refers to the expression "full and by. " This expression meant that the boat was traveling against the direction of the wind. This was first a nautical term that then made its way into everyday conversation. The other expression large is a nautical term that means that wind and boat are traveling in the same direction. If you combine, by and large, it would mean that the wind is "large" was its own term used to mean that the wind was traveling in the same direction as the boat. Therefore, by saying "by and large", a sailor was suggesting that the wind is coming from all directions.

Example: The number of graduating students has been by and large even during the pandemic.

By hook or by crook

Meaning: Something will be obtained by whatever means is necessary, regardless if it is proper or legal.

Origin: This idiom dates back to the Medieval English Laws that state that peasants can use tree branches if they are not able to get branches of the three with the use of a crook or a billhook.

Example: I'm going to get the limited edition bag, whether it's by hook or by crook.

By the gross

Meaning: In large numbers or amounts.

Origin: In the past, gross was often synonymous with a twelve dozen. This is because the expression was taken from the French phrase "grosse douzaine", which literally means 'large dozen'.

Example: The success of the person does not measure how much by the gross he is earning.

By the skin of your teeth

Meaning: To escape an undesired outcome narrowly; to achieve something by a narrow margin

Origin: This idiom comes from the Book of Job. Job was a person who was suffering from tragedies and unfortunate events. But one good trait of Job is that he possessed a strong faith in God. Despite all things, he remained faithful. In Job 19:20, Job speaks, "I am nothing but skin and bones; I have escaped only by the skin of my teeth".Thus, how the idiom came to be.

Example: You were able to make it through by the skin of your teeth.

Call it a day

Meaning: This means to stop doing something for the day, for example, work, either temporarily or to give it up completely.

Origins: The expression was originally "call it half a day". This expression was first recorded in 1838. The context means to leave one's place of work before the working day is over. "Call it a day" came later, in 1919.

Example: Let's call it a day! Everyone seems tired from the grueling activities.

Call of duty

Meaning: A feeling that you must do something because it's a duty.; also refer to the shooting game of the same title.

Origin: There is no clear origin of this idiomatic expression. However, it is often referred to the feeling that one gets whenever they talk about their country. It makes them feel obligated to do something for their country.

Example: Korean men have to enlist because it's their call of duty.

Call someone's bluff

Meaning: To challenge to prove one's claim, when they are likely attempting to deceive

Origin: This idiom was inspired by poker. Bluffing is a technique in which a person bluffs that he has the best card while hoping his opponent will fold.

Example: One way to call someone's bluff is by willingly losing everything that you thought was right or wrong.

Call the shots

Meaning: To be in charge of what is happening and what should happen

Origin: This expression was military slang. It was often used in military marksmanship training. It was first cited in the 1960s. If a marksman is able to get a successful shot, it would be called "his shot."

Example: My mother is the one that calls the shots in the family.

Can't carry a tune in a bucket

Meaning: Tone-deaf and unable to sing the simplest melodies properly

Origin: This expression was used in the early 1920's in the book Emmett Lawler by Jim Tully. He wrote: "Emmett burst forth in song, but his comrade punched him in the side and said, 'Lord Sakes, shut up, you can't carry a tune in a bucket.'"

Example: It sounds so bad! He can't carry a tune in a bucket!

Can't do something to save my life

Meaning: Incapable of doing anything

Origins: It was first used in a book by Anthony Trollope in 1848. In his writing, he wrote, "If it was to save my life and theirs, I can't get up small talk for the rector and his curate."

Example: She doesn't know anything at all. She can't do anything to save her life!

Carte blanche

Meaning: Blank Paper

Origin: This expression was adapted from French which means "blank paper." But in some dictionaries, it is also referred to as the freedom to give power to another person.

Example: A masterpiece starts as a carte blanche before the artist adds his touch.

Cat among the pigeons

Meaning: Refers to saying or doing something that annoys people

Origin: Originally, this expression was taken from a British term during the colonization of India. There was a certain practice where people put a wild cat inside a cage filled with pigeons. People will then bet on how many pigeons a cat can take down with one swipe.

Example: He was the cat among the pigeons. I can't stand his presence in my class.

Cat got your tongue

Meaning: When a person is at loss for words

Origin: The first origin of this idiom refers to a whip called "cat-o-nine-tails". This whip was used by the English Navy. Many victims were rendered speechless after they were flogged with a "cat-o-nine-tails."

Example: I think a cat got my tongue after seeing the big surprise for my birthday.

Caught red-handed

Meaning: To be caught in the act of doing something wrong.

Origin: This idiom was first used in 1432 in Scotland. It refers to an old English law. This law states that the person who has butchered an animal that he doesn't own will be punished. The way to convict this person is to catch him with the animal's blood on his hand.

Example: Sean was caught red-handed sneaking cookies from the cookie jar.

Caught with one's pants down

Meaning: Caught in the act of doing the crime

Origin: This expression was originally taken from the assassination of Emperor Caracalla who was killed when relieving himself on the road.

Example: I caught my dog with his pants down. He was the one shredding all the rolls of toilet paper in the bathroom.

Change gear

Meaning: Begin to move or act differently, usually more rapidly

Origin: This expression was taken from motorcycles and vehicles. To speed up, most motorcycles would change their gear.

Example: Let's change gears and try again.

Change one's tune

Meaning: Reversing one's behavior

Origin: This idiom dates back to the 1300's, when itinerant minstrels had to alter their songs to suit their audiences. It was only in 1808 that this expression was used in English Literature.

Example: Don't expect him to change his tune overnight.

Chasing one's own tail

Meaning: Doing a lot of things simultaneously without completing anything,

Origin: This expression was likened to a puppy or kitten playing with their own tail. It cannot achieve anything by simply chasing its tail.

Example: She was chasing her own tail. She had so much to do but accomplished very little.

Cheap as chips

Meaning: The price is low and cheap.

Origin: In British English, chips are synonymous with French fries in the US. It is very common in the UK that chips are sold cheap.

Example: Dresses and clothes at Target are cheap as chips.

Cheek by jowl

Meaning: In close intimacy; close together

Origin: Originally, this expression was first coined during the 14th century. It was coined from the idea of being nice and close to people, hence the expression "cheke by cheke". However, in the 16th century, the expression changed from cheke to cheke to cheke to jowl. Only the expression changed but the meaning remains the same.

Example: They were able to live cheek by jowl with their estranged family.

Cheesed off

Meaning: Fed up

Origin: This expression's origin still remains unknown. However, this expression was taken in the same context of brassed off, ticked off, pissed off.

Example: They are all cheesed off because of what is currently happening.

Chew the fat

Meaning: Mindless chatter, gossipings.

Origin: In the past, farmers and sailors would save the fat rind and serve it during informal gatherings.

Example: Sierra and Athena were chewing the fat when I passed by them.

Chicken scratches

Meaning: Bad handwriting

Origin: This idiomatic expression was inspired by how chickens would scratch the dirt to look for food. This expression was used because the scratches seemed very similar to children's bad handwriting.

Example: I can't help but complain that I am reading chicken scratches.

Chill pill

Meaning: Soothing and calming; Imaginary pill to make someone relax.

Origin: This expression was first used in the 1800s. Chill pill used to be a medicine to help with chills caused by fever. However, the word "chill pill" was then used to describe the medicines that were prescribed to children who were believed to suffer from ADHD. This chill pill was used to calm these children.

Example: You need to take a chill pill and take the time off to rest your mind.

Chopped liver

Meaning: One that is insignificant or not worth considering

Origin: This expression was inspired by different cuisines. In the past, the liver was often considered a side dish and not the main dish.

Example: This file is full of chopped liver.

Chow down

Meaning: To eat quickly

Origin: The word chow used to be a Chinese slang for food. During the 20th century, this expression made it to the USA after World War II. It was often used as military slang for eating.

Example: Milo had to chow down his food before the bus arrived.

Clean bill of health

Meaning: Healthy

Origin:" Clean bill of health" was first coined during the 1800s. Before traveling, the crew of the ship must be examined by a health official to ensure that they don't have anything infectious. Both the sailor and the ship were given a clean bill of health. This bill must be submitted before docking at the next port.

Example: She was given a clean bill of health. She is ready to discharge.

Clear the decks

Meaning: Prepare for an event or course of action by dealing with anything that might hinder progress.

Origin: However it originally was used when ships were preparing for battle and sailors would remove objects on the deck of the ship.

Example: We should clear the decks before the guest arrives.

Close but no cigar

Meaning: Be very close to accomplishing a goal but fall short

Origin: Dated back during the early to mid-twentieth century when cigars used to be a grand prize in many events.

Example: You were almost there. So close but no cigar.

Close call

Meaning: A narrow escape from disaster

Origin: Taken from a sports event, this expression was first coined in the late 1800s. Although it was not fully stated what happened at that time, an official was forced to make a decision to avoid a possible disaster.

Example: Miki had a close call but thank God she made it out alive.

Cold hearted

Meaning: Someone unkind and possibly rude; someone who doesn't"show emotions towards other people

Origin: This expression was taken from the idea in medicine where cold hearted is signified as someone dead. In the 17th century, this expression was then used to refer to someone who doesn't really show their emotions towards others.

Example: Many people often taunt Camille for being cold hearted.

Cold shoulder

Meaning: Disrespect, ignore, or dismiss another person's presence.

Origin: This expression dates back to the Medieval ages. Unwanted guests are often served cold mutton while the welcomed ones get a warm and well-cooked meal.

Example: She gave me a cold shoulder after I forgot my promise yesterday.

Cold sweat

Meaning: A condition where a person would sweat due to extreme fear and nervousness.

Origin: The origin of this expression is currently unknown. However, it was believed that this expression was first used between the late 1500s to 1700s AD. It referred to a phenomena of feeling the chills and sweating when one is extremely anxious or nervous.

Example: I broke into a cold sweat while waiting for her reply to my marriage proposal.

Comb through

Meaning: Examine closely or check thoroughly.

Origin: It was taken from the idea of combing through every bit of scalp on a person's head.

Example: Make sure you comb through your answer, you might have missed some blanks.

Come out of one's shell

Meaning: To stop being shy and begin to confidently show your real character and feelings

Origin: This phrase was inspired by a snail or a turtle who often hides in their shells when there are strangers around them.

Example: It took a lot of time for Kiara to come out of her shell. Now, she is a happy little girl.

Come out swinging

Meaning: To enter the confrontation with the intent to clash ideas or objectives.

Origin: This sports idiom is related to boxing when two opponents leave their corners swinging jabs to challenge their opponent to make the first move.

Example: Designs were coming out swinging when they were talking about the new ideas for the fair.

Come to blows

Meaning: To start fighting; Used to refer to the beginning of a fight between two groups or parties

Origin: This expression was taken from the 18th century. It was first cited in the novel of Charles Dickens called "Nicholas Nickleby" and it was also cited in Thomas Hardy's The Return of the Native. However, this expression was inspired by professional boxing where pugilists would come to blows when they fought.

Example: They almost came to blows at the basketball court today.

Coming out of the woodwork

Meaning: Unwanted people coming over without your knowledge.

Origin: In the past, this phrase was used to refer to bugs and other vermin coming out of the walls of the houses. It was then likened to unwanted people coming over during the 1950s.

Example: Unexpected people are coming out of the woodwork after hearing that my teacher has returned.

Connect the dots

Meaning: Figure out the whole situation by using all the gathered information.

Origin: This idiom originated from the puzzle called dot-to-dot. In this puzzle, people have to connect the dots with corresponding numbers for them to get the whole idea of the picture.

Example: You don't have to read everything in the story. You can connect the dots together to know what happened in the book.

Crocodile tears

Meaning: Superficial or false tears.

Origin: Centuries ago, people assumed that crocodiles would shed tears while devouring their prey. But the reality is, crocodiles would shed tears to moisten their eyes after being out for so long.

Example: Dana cried crocodile tears when Bruno left.

Cross the line

Meaning: Behave in a way that is not acceptable.: Overstep a boundary, standard, or rule.

Origin: This expression was an ancient maritime ritual when a crew member or passengers crossed the equator for the first time, the ship held a ceremony to commemorate this occasion.

Example: He crossed the line and now they have been arguing since they arrived from the party.

Cut a dash

Meaning: Be stylish or impressive in your dress or behavior.

Origin: This expression was originally taken from the word "dash" which literally means "showy appearance." However, this expression was then used as an adjective which is the word "dashing."

Example: We all have our own way of how to cut a dash.

Cut a deal

Meaning: Come to an arrangement, especially in business; make a deal.

Origin: This expression was coined after the expression " a share of profits."

Example: It's time to go and cut a deal with the Jones.

Cut and run

Meaning: Avoid a difficult situation by leaving abruptly

Origin: This nautical idiom was used in the early 1700s. Cut and run was an expression used when ships were under attack. Instead of pulling the anchors up, the captain asked the crew to cut the ropes that hold the anchors and escape. This expression was first used in 1861 by Charles Dickens in his novel Great Expectations.

Example: Maybe we should cut and run before everything turns out bad.

Cut somebody some slack

Meaning: Don't be so critical

Origin: The origin of this phrase was an allusion to docking ships. When sailors would say "give me some slack" during this era, it means that they want you to loosen the ropes. In 1855, the phrase was then used in the book "My Bondage and Freedom" wherein it was reworded to "cut slack for."

Example: Cut somebody some slack when you feel that they had a hard day.

Cut the cord

Meaning: To end a connection with someone

Origin: This idiom was taken from the idea of cutting the umbilical cord of the fetus after birth. The umbilical cord was the baby's source of oxygen and nutrients before it was born. Figuratively, this expression alludes to the newborn babies' reliance on the nutrition from the cord.

Example: Sometimes, we have to cut the cord with the people that cause us grief.

Cutting edge

Meaning: A trait that makes it better against its competitors; latest features.

Origin: This expression was taken from the idea "having the edge over" in the world of business. Cutting the edge through the launch of something that is bigger or better is often done regularly in parties.

Example: It comes with a cutting-edge design.

Damsel in distress

Meaning: Talk about a female that needs to be rescued

Origin: This expression is taken from the French word "demoiselle". But this expression was inspired by Greek tragedies where women are considered fragile and need to be rescued.

Example: Sienna looked like a damsel in distress stuck in the middle of an argument.

Dance attendance on

Meaning: Do your utmost to please someone by attending to all their needs or requests.

Origin: This expression was originally referred to as "someone kicking their heels". This expression was used to summon or ask a person to see them.

Example: They were always on dance attendance with us just to get our approval on their project.

Dawn on (someone)

Meaning: The truth is slowly becoming clearer.

Origin: This expression was likened to the dawning of the day after a long period of darkness. It was then used figuratively during the 1830s.

Example: The information slowly dawned on them as they realized that John had been right all along.

Day in and day out

Meaning: Constant practice; every day without an exception

Origin: This expression was first added in the Webster dictionary in 1913 but has been used in earlier printings since 1895.

Example: To become the best artist, you need to practice day in and day out.

Day of reckoning

Meaning: The time when an unpleasant situation has to be dealt with.

D)

Origin: This expression refers to the Day of Judgment in the Bible. It talks about the time when God answers the question of its people.

Example: Today is the day of reckoning. We will finally know if we have passed or failed the test.

Days of wine and roses

Meaning: The carefree days with no responsibility to worry about.

Origin: This expression was taken from the poem Vitae Summa Brevis by Ernest Dowson where they talk about youthful days that one doesn't have to worry about.

Example: Gone are the days of wine and roses where I don't have to worry about everything.

Dead in the water

Meaning: Without any chance of success; stalled.

Origin: This nautical expression was coined way before engines were invented. During the early era of exploration, ships were solely dependent on winds to help them navigate the sea. If there are no winds, the ship is considered dead in the water because of its unmoving stance. Hence, the expression "dead in the water"

Example: It was dead in the water, we lost the first half of the game.

Dead on your feet

Meaning: Extremely tired.

Origin: This expression was inspired by the phrase "dead tired," which was an expression used to exaggerate or express the feeling of exhaustion.

Example: You look dead on your feet, what happened to you?

Dead to the world

Meaning: Sleeping soundly.

Origin: This expression used to mean "forgiven of sin" which was taken from the book titled "Dead to the World, in Sin and Atonement" by Klara Bauer in 1874. But now it is used to describe people who are sleeping soundly.

Example: He was dead to the world after a strenuous long day.

Delusions of grandeur

Meaning: A false impression of your own importance.

Origin: This expression was an English translation of the French phrase "folie de grandeur" which was used in the late 19th century.

Example: Your delusions of grandeur will get you nowhere.

Dice with death

Meaning: Take serious risks.

Origin: In this context, the word "dice" is often referred to as "playing a game of chance" This expression was first coined in the mid-20th century. It likened death to a game of dice. This expression is also used for racing drivers who are fond of driving at a fast speed.

Example: If you want to play dice with death, go ahead. But leave me out of it.

Die in harness

Meaning: Die before retirement.

Origin: This expression was comparing a working person and a horse in a harness who is plowing the fields

Example: We all die in harnesses if we forget to take care of ourselves.

Die in the last-ditch

Meaning: Die desperately defending something; die fighting to the last extremity.

Origin: This expression was taken from the remake of King William III when he was asked if his country had lost the war. He responded as 'There is one way never to see it lost, and that is to die in the last-ditch.'

Examples: She will die in the last-ditch just to protect her country.

Die with your boots on

Meaning: Die while actively occupied.

Origin: "Die with your boots on" was apparently first used in the late 19th century for the deaths of cowboys and others in the American West who were killed in gun battles or hanged.

Example: If you don't pay attention while crossing the street, you will die with your boots on.

Die-hard

Meaning: Disappear or change slowly

Origin: This expression was first coined in the battle of Albuera in 1811. It was coined by Commander Willia Inglis and exhorted his men to be "die-hard". Because of their heroism, they were coined "die-hards."

Example: Radical views will eventually die hard.

Dig a pit for

Meaning: Try to trap.

Origin: This is a common biblical metaphor: for example, in Jeremiah 18:20 we find 'they have dug a pit for my soul'.

Example: You are going to dig a pit for yourself if you don't pay attention in class.

Dig in your heels

Meaning: Resist stubbornly; refuse to give in.

Origin: The image here is of a horse or other animal obstinately refusing to be led or ridden forwards. Dig in your heels is the commonest form, but dig in your toes and dig in your feet are also found.

Example: She needs to dig her heels about her decision.

Dig one's own grave

Meaning: To do something that will lead you to your downfall

Origin: This expression dates back to the middle half of the 19th century but was first used figuratively in 1829.

Example: Mina was digging her own grave with her decisions.

Dire straits

Meaning: In danger

Origin: This expression came to be with the word "dire". In Latin, the word dire is often associated with dreadful, terrible, and dangerous. If you pair it up with traveling to troubled waters, then it connotes danger in traveling on the sea.

Example: Jean can be in dire straits right now! We should have never left her alone!

Dog days

Meaning: The hottest days of the year

Origin: This expression was taken from the Roman phrase "dies caniculares." Romans believed that during the dog days, the star Sirius would rise and give off heat alongside the sun. With these two, they are able to produce too much heat on earth.

Example: Dog days are the most annoying days of the year.

Don't cry over spilled milk

Meaning: Not to worry over unfortunate events that have happened and can not be changed.

Origin: This expression probably originated during the 1650s when milk was one of the most expensive commodities in the market. People would often cry when milk is spilled.

Example: Don't cry over spilled milk, there is nothing we can do about it.

Don't have a leg to stand on

Meaning: Someone is figuratively crippled and can't stand on their own feet.

Origin: This expression was taken from the book Reason and Religion, or the Certain Rule of Faith by Edward Worsley, 1672 on page 332: "Fail to do this and your Assertion hath not so much as one leg to stand on, besides fancy, or something worse."

Example: She doesn't have a leg to stand on after what happened.

Don't judge a book by its cover

Meaning: Do not judge someone by the way he or she looks or dresses.

Origin: This expression was first used in George Eliot's The Mill on the Floss, published in England in 1860. One character used this expression when they were discussing a book called The Political History of the Devil by Daniel Defoe.

Example: Don't judge the book by its cover, there are a lot of things that you don't know about them.

Don't sweat the small stuff

Meaning: Do not worry about things that are not important.

Origin: This expression was coined by the author Dr. Richard Carson in his book called Don't Sweat the Small Stuff...and it's all Small Stuff.

Example: Don't sweat the small stuff. It's going to be alright.

Done to a turn

Meaning: Perfectly cook

Origin: This expression originated during the Medieval era when meat was often cooked in spits being turned over by an open fire.

Example: My fried chicken was done to a turn.

Don't rock the boat

Meaning: Disturb the situation

Meaning: This expression is inspired by navigation. However, it was first phrased by William Bryan. To quote, he said, "The man who rocks the boat ought to be stoned when he gets back onshore." This expression was expressed in his opinion against the Hues Corporation.

Example: Don't rock the boat! We are yet to solve the current problem.

Double take

Meaning: Surprise at something that leads you to look at it again; delayed reaction.

Origin: Originally, this expression was coined during the 1920s. It came from the idea that directors would often check the recording a second time to see if anything needed to be re-done

Example: Max did a double take at Celine to make sure it was her that he was looking at.

Down and out

Meaning: Unconcious

Origin: This expression originated from boxing. Down and out happens when an opponent knocks down the other player who is unable to finish the match because of unconsciousness.

Example: She was down and out as soon as they arrived home.

Down the hatch

Meaning: Drinking or making a toast

Origin: This naval idiom is taken from the opening of the ship called the hatch where they put all the cargo. This naval idiom was used figuratively to describe how liquor goes down the throat.

Example: A shot of tequila, down the hatch.

Drain the swamp

Meaning: Removing the practice of corruption.

Origin: The origin of this expression was based on the practice of draining the swamp to lessen mosquitoes from breeding and fight off malaria. It was only used figuratively when Winfield R. Gaylord first used this expression figuratively. He referred to this expression about removing the source of corruption in the government.

Example: The women's movement aims to drain the swamp in our government.

Draw a line in the sand

Meaning: Refers to determining a physical point at which one may proceed no further;

Origin: It was inspired by the expedition of Francisco Pizarro. Pizarro drew the line in the sand and talked about poverty and Peru. He referred to Peru as an island where the treasure lies.

Example: Darwin drew a line in the sand when they divided the basketball court for practice.

Dressed to the nines

Meaning: Flashily and smartly attired.

Origin: This expression used to be synonymous with the words "almost perfect". In the past, the number 9 was used as a superlative in describing clothes or other things.

Example: Alicia was dressed to the nines for her senior prom.

Drifting through life

Meaning: Without a purpose in life

Origin: This expression is taken from the idea of being adrift in the sea where you are at the mercy of the currents and winds.

Example: I was drifting through life. It took me years to find my purpose.

Drive a hard bargain

Meaning: This means demanding that the other party in a transaction settle for less than asked or expected in exchange for a product or service.

Origin: This expression was first used in 1819 in one of the cases handled by William P. Mason where he said: "But there is a wide distinction between such a case and the case where a father, with a view to favoring his son, and not to drive a hard bargain with him, makes a small deduction from his ordinary prices..."

Example: The buyers drive a hard bargain to ensure that they get the property.

Drive someone up the wall

Meaning: Extremely annoying

Origin: This expression was taken from an idea of locking two people in one room with no way of escape. Aside from that, the other person in the room is annoying the other person to the point that he would climb walls to escape.

Example: The loud horns of cars are driving me up the wall.

Drop someone or something like a hot potato

Meaning: Quickly abandon someone or something

Origin: The word "drop" is used to define the figurative sense of the 'end of a social acquaintance with someone.' The word "hot potato" can be used independently. It also refers to controversial and awkward issues that no one would have to deal with.

Example: He dropped her like a hot potato.

Drop the ball

Meaning: Creating mistakes that can cause problems for other people.

Origin: Originally taken from football wherein the ball was fumbled and cost the team a huge disadvantage.

Example: She dropped the ball and now they have to do everything all over again.

Dry run

Meaning: A rehearsal before the actual performance.

Origin: This expression was taken from rehearsals done by the fire department. During these rehearsals they don't use water. They keep the rehearsals dry.

Example: How about we do a dry run before the actual launching?

Dutch courage

Meaning: Foolish courage

Origin: This expression was taken from the practice or a habit of many English soldiers who would drink Jenever and do some kind of display.

Example: You don't need Dutch courage to tell them that you broke that important vase.

Dyed in the wool

Meaning: Totally committed to one's opinions

Origin: This expression was taken from the idea of dying raw wool with vegetable dye. In Medieval times, this method often took too long but the color in the wool permeated every fiber. It is often used to describe a politician with a strong set of beliefs.

Example: They were dyed in the wool and are 100% ready to support his beliefs.

Early bird

Meaning: Person who arrives early or acts before the usual time

Origin: This expression was taken from the proverb "The early bird catches the worm" which means that the person who wakes up early or starts early can gain an advantage over others.

Example: Sara is one of the early birds in our class.

Early doors

Meaning: Early on, especially in a game or contest.

Origin: Apparently this expression arose with reference to a period of admission to a music hall ending sometime before the start of the performance and giving a better choice of seating.

Example: She did a lot of practice, early doors.

Earworm

Meaning: A tune or song stuck in your head.

Origin: This expression was first published in Mark Twain's A Literary Nightmare" It talks about a musical phrase that can only be erased by simply passing it to another person. The actual word 'earworm' was only used in the 1978 novel "Flyaway."

Example: Bam Bam is the current earworm running in my head.

Easy as falling off a log

Meaning: Very easy.

Origin: This expression was originally a mid-19th-century American one, but it is now in general use. It was used around the year 1880 by Mark Twain in the alternative form of rolling off a log.

Example: Math is an easy subject. It is as easy as falling off a log.

Easy come, easy go

Meaning: It often refers to money and how easy it is to buy things with it.

Origin: This expression was first used in a printed article in January 1868. The article was titled

'Pittsburg': "Exemplifications these of the old adage, 'Easy come, easy go.'"

Example: Easy come, easy go, the rich can easily buy things as they go.

Eat humble pie

Meaning: To admit you were wrong or apologize.

Origin: In the 14th century, hunting was one of the popular sports in Europe. The lords of the manor would often celebrate with a post-hunt feast. The lords would often get the finest cuts of meat. People of lower stature were given the entrails, heart, and liver. These internal parts were given the name umbles. Umbles used to be baked into a pie. That's how the expression came to be.

Example: You need to eat humble pie and learn from your mistake.

Eating crow

Meaning: Accepting one's mistake after being corrected.

Origin: This expression's origin was inspired by a story published in SanFrancisco's Daily Evening Picayune where they talk about a simple farmer in Lake Mahopac, New York.

Example: He was eating crow after he was caught cheating.

Economical with the truth

Meaning: Used euphemistically to describe a person or statement that lies or deliberately withholds information.

Origin: This expression was coined by Edmund Burke when he was observing Mark Twain. He wrote 'Truth is the most valuable thing we have. Let us economize it' (Following the Equator, 1897). This expression was then popularized during the Spycatcher Trial in the New South Wales Supreme Court.

Example: She tried to be economical with the truth. She doesn't want to hurt her feelings.

Egg someone on

Meaning: To goad or get someone angry

Origin: This expression was first cited during the mid-16th century. It was often associated with the idiom "rotten eggs."

Example: If you keep on egging on someone, you will definitely be punched in the face.

Elephant in the room

Meaning: An important topic or issue that everyone is acutely aware of, but isn't discussing due to embarrassment or sensitivity

Origin: This idiomatic expression was taken from the fable 'The Inquisitive Man' by Ivan Krylov. It tells a story of a man visiting a museum noticing all kinds of small and important things but failing to see the giant elephant.

Example: They failed to address the elephant in the room, again.

Every man for himself

Meaning: everyone must take care of themselves and their own interests and safety.

Origin: This expression was first used during Medieval times. However, its variation grew from the mid-16th century onwards. There is no clear origin for this expression but it has been used literally since then.

Example: It's every man for himself when we talk about survival.

Every nook and cranny

Meaning: Search in every available space

Origin: This expression was first coined in the 14th century. The word nooks used to mean a distant corner while cranny defined a crack or gap. If you combine these two expressions it means that you need to find the object in every distant corner and tiny gap.

Example: I have searched every nook and cranny and yet I still can't find where Griselda is hiding.

Extend an olive branch

Meaning: To extend or offer peace. Propose a treaty.

Origin: In the Bible, the olive branch is considered the universal symbol of peace. In Genesis 8:11, a dove brought back an olive branch to signify that Noah and his family were safe from the flood.

Example: Sierra is trying her best to extend an olive branch to her estranged family.

Eye candy

Meaning: Attractive visually but uninteresting in other ways

Origin: This expression appeared in the late 70s. During that time, it referred to someone who is pretty but not educated.

Example: Damien looks like eye candy to me.

Eyes down!

Meaning: be ready to concentrate fully on the matter before you.

Origin: This expression was coined as an injunction to give your full attention to your card when a game of bingo was about to start.

Example: Eyes down everyone! Let's start preparing the next concept for our new marketing campaign.

F)

Face the music

Meaning: Owning up to an unpleasant situation; accepting the truth

Origin: Based on practice from the Old British Military where they would play the drums when someone is court-martialed.

Example: We all have to face the music after the divorce.

Facing a strong headwind

Meaning: force or influence that hinders the progress of certain things

Origin: This expression was taken from the early era of navigation. A strong headwind is a force that causes ships to alter their course. This expression is often used in business.

Example: Today, we are facing a strong headwind because of the pandemic.

Fair and square

Meaning: Honest in one's dealings.

Origin: This expression originated in the late 16th century when the word "square" was defined as someone who is an honest dealer. It was used by George Puttenham to describe Aristotle in the article Arte of English Poesie. He wrote: "[Aristotle] termeth a constant-minded man—a square man.".

Example: I won the game fair and square.

Fall (or land) on your feet

Meaning: Achieve a fortunate outcome in a difficult situation.

Origin: Inspired by the fact that cats can land on their feet regardless of how high they fall or jump from.

Example: I am glad that we were able to land on our feet.

Fall from grace

Meaning: Someone withdrawn or removed from his current position

Origin: This expression was first used in the Bible in the writings of St. Paul in Galatians 5:4. He wrote, "Christ has become of no effect unto you, whosoever of you are justified by the law; ye are fallen from grace."

Example: The royal family fell from grace after the revolution.

Fall in (or into) line

Meaning: Conform with others or with accepted behavior.

Origin: This phrase originally referred to soldiers arranging themselves into military formation.

Example: If one person makes a good example, others will fall in line.

Fall into place

Meaning: Describes a certain situation that leads all the factors into the most unexpected situation.

Origin: There were no specific origins from this expression. However, this expression was said to be dated during the early 19th century. It was only at the end of the century that the definition of this idiom was determined in the biographical work of Newell Dunbar titled Philip Brooks, the Man, the Preacher, and the Author.

Example: All the hard work you have done will help things fall into place.

Fall on one's sword

Meaning: To take responsibility even if it causes harm or for the greater good.

Origin: This phrase was derived from soldiers committing suicide by falling on their swords during the ancient wars in Israel.

Example: You should not fall on your sword if you weren't responsible for what happened.

Famous last words

Meaning: An ironic comment on or reply to an overconfident assertion that may well soon be proved wrong by events.

Origin: It was coined around the mid-20th century when it was used as a catchphrase in the military.

Example: Do you have any famous last words before leaving this house?

Fan the flames

Meaning: Make the situation become worse.

Origin: This idiom is an allusion of blowing or fanning the fire. By doing so, it helps to increase the intensity of the flames. This expression originated in the mid-1800s and was first cited in the Old Curiosity Shop by Charles Dickens.

Example: I didn't mean to fan the flames.

Fat chance

Meaning: Incredibly unlikely. It is related to the expression "slim chance" which means the same thing.

Origins: The origins of this expression are unclear, but the use of the word "fat" is likely to be a sarcastic version of saying "slim chance".

Example: It's a fat chance that she would be able to hit the bull's eye with her current stance.

Feast of reason

Meaning: Intellectual talk.

Origin: This expression was inspired by the poet Alexander Pope's description of a congenial conversation about the limitation of Horace. He wrote 'The feast of reason and the flow of soul'.

Example: They are huddled in the corner having a feast of reason about the current pandemic.

Feeding frenzy

Meaning: An episode of frantic competition or rivalry for something.

Origin: This expression was taken from a group of sharks or piranha feeding on prey.

Example: They were all stuck in a feeding frenzy after the announcement of the new album.

Feeling blue

Meaning: Sad

Origin: This expression originated from a certain practice on a ship. If a captain or an officer dies at sea, the crew will paint the ship's hull with a blue band and a blue flag will be raised on the mast.

Example: Melissa was feeling blue after hearing the news.

Feeling groggy

Meaning: It means you are weak and unable to think clearly or walk correctly, usually because of tiredness or illness.

Origin: This expression was first coined by Admiral Edward Verno who likes wearing grogam jackets. He was even given the nickname Old Grog for it.

Example: After taking my nap, it always left me feeling groggy and on edge.

Feeling one's oats

Meaning: Feeling robust or energetic

Origin: This phrase was derived from horses who were well-loved by their owners. Well-fed horses would often perk up when they saw their owners carrying their food into the stables.

Example: The children were feeling their oats after they saw all the candies they received from trick or treating.

Feeling the heat

Meaning: Encountering an uncomfortable situation due to undue pressure.

Origin: This expression was first coined from the certain idea of getting too close to the fire has a possible unpleasant result.

Example: I was feeling the heat of the argument between them. So, I left them to get some coffee.

Feeling under the weather

Meaning: Sick; not feeling well

Origin: This expression refers to sailors who get seasick during rough weather. They would often hide beneath the bow. This way, it will counter the effects of the bad weather on them.

Example: Ces is feeling under the weather. She is currently resting in her room.

Feet of clay

Meaning: A weakness perceived in someone held in high regard

Origin: This expression was taken from the Book of Daniel. This idiomatic expression came to be when Daniel interpreted one of Nebuchadnezzar's dreams about a statue with both iron and clay feet. This dream was interpreted that the kingdom of Nebuchadnezzar would be great but divided in the long run.

Example: No matter how famous the person is, they all have feet of clay just like you and me.

Fend off

Meaning: Distance or defend oneself from a possible attack

Origin: This expression refers to the fenders on the vessel. In order to avoid possible collisions, your ship must have several fenders to help you minimize the damage on your ship

Example: They fend off her suitors, especially the questionable ones.

Fetch and carry

Meaning: Go backward and forwards bringing things to someone in a servile fashion.

Origin: This expression was originally referred to as a hunting dog retrieving the game that has been shot.

Example: He made me fetch and carry his stuff from the car.

Fight like cat and dog

Meaning: Argue violently all the time; A situation where two people are continuously arguing or fighting with each other about a particular issue

Origin: The origin of this expression was quite ambiguous. However, it is believed that this expression was related to the relationship between cats and dogs in the early 1600s. It is common knowledge that dogs and cats are natural enemies.

Example: Alex and Sandra often fight like a cat and dog over petty things.

Fight nail and tooth

Meaning: To fight fiercely

Origin: This idiom stemmed from the ancient Latin expression "toto corpore atque omnibus ungulis" which translated to "all the body and every nail."

Example: Parents would fight nail and tooth for their child's best interest.

First light

Meaning: Dawn; The time when the first light in the morning appears.

Origin: This expression was first used in the 1700s when people didn't really have gadgets to help them tell time. They would often refer to dawn as the first light or the earliest part of the morning.

Example: They have to leave at first light.

First rate

Meaning: Of the best quality; of high quality

Origin: This naval idiom was first used during the reign of King Henry VII. During his time, naval ships were graded into six rates. Firstrate was often given to the biggest and well-armed ships while the sixth rate was given to a small ship with less armory.

Example: We have enough first rate organza to make a fine dress.

Fit as a fiddle

Meaning: In very good health

Origin: In the 17th century the word "fit" wasn't associated with the word "healthy" but suitable. While the word "fiddle" is another term used to describe a violin. Originally this idiom meant " a suitable person" But the expression "fit as a fiddle" was associated with health in 1601 in the comedy play titled "Englishmen for My Money" by William Haughton.

Example: Don't worry, mother. I am fit as a fiddle!

Fits like a glove

Meaning: Good fit; tailored-fit

Origin: It was first cited by physician Tobias G. Smollett in his article "The Exposition of Humphry Clinker." He used the expression to describe the fit of his boots to the fit of his gloves.

Example: This dress fits me like a glove.

Fits the bill

Meaning: Everything is all good

Origin: This expression refers to the Bill of Lading which is a contract between the seller and the shipper. It contains all the information about the goods to be shipped and their condition. Once the products are delivered, the buyer will tell the seller that the products fit the bill.

Example: Everything looks ok. It fits the bill.

Five will get you ten

Meaning: Chances are good

Origin: This idiomatic expression first began in the early 20th century. It was first used in betting parlance. It was written in a printed reference where they say 'Five will get you ten!' instead of saying 'Do you want to bet on it?'

Example: Five will get you ten, and Black Beauty will win the race.

Flash in the pan

Meaning: Someone offers a lot but delivers nothing

Origin: This expression has been used since the late 17th century during the California Gold Rush. Flash in the pan has been used in many contexts in printed references and plays.

Example: He flashes in the pan during the football game. Sad to say, I am very disappointed with the outcome of the game.

Fly high

Meaning: Be very successful; prosper.

Origin: This expression is the verb of a noun called "high flyer." This noun refers to a person who is ambitious and successful at what he does.

Example: We all want to fly high and achieve our dreams.

Fly in the face of

Meaning: To go diametrically against an accepted belief or practice.

Origin: This metaphorical expression was used to allude to a mother hen flying into the face of a predator that is threatening her chicks.

Example: To fly in the face of this tradition has brought people raising their brows.

Fly off the handle

Meaning: To become suddenly enraged.

Origin: This idiom referred to the badly made ax during the 1800s. If you swing these axes too hard, the ax heads will fly off the handle.

Example: My mother flew off the handle after learning about my failing grade.

Fly the nest

Meaning: Children who are leaving home to start living on their own.

Origin: This expression was taken from the image of fledglings learning to fly out of the nest.

Example: Her parents were saddened by her decision to fly the nest.

Food for thought

Meaning: An idea or subject that you can think about.

Origin: This expression dates back during the French Revolution. During the Era of Reason, people shared their opinions and ideas of the many religious beliefs that were taught. It was then when people started to question the existence of many things.

Example: I think the planning team has some food for thought for us.

Fool's gold

Meaning Deceptively beautiful

Origin: Fool's gold is a popular name for gold that a lot of people often mistake gold for. Oftentimes, these stones are pyrite and chalcopyrite.

Example: Do not be fooled by this fool's gold. You might be disappointed to know its real form.

Footloose and fancy-free

Meaning: Free from care or responsibility; unattached and single

Origin: Footloose and fancy-free was a naval expression used during olden days. The foot referred to in the expression refers to the bottom part of the sail that is connected to the boom. When the winds blow strong, the foot is detached from the boom, which becomes footloose. Footloose sails would flap around wherever the wind would blow. Hence the expression footloose and fancy-free was created.

Example: He was all footloose and fancy-free when he left home.

For donkey's years

Meaning: For a very long time

Origin: This expression doesn't really talk about the donkey's years but ears. This expression was used to liken time with the ears of the donkey.

Example: We thought you and Jim had been married for a donkey's year.

Forbidden fruit

Meaning: A thing that is desired all the more because it is not allowed.

Origin: This expression was taken from the Bible. It was first found in the creation story of the Garden of Eden where Adam and Eve were told to not eat the forbidden apple.

Example: Wealth is the forbidden fruit that many of us seek but not all of us can have.

Foregone conclusion

Meaning: Bound to happen

Origin: This idiom was first coined in 1604 by Shakespeare in his play Othello III where he said "But this denoted a foregone conclusion" as a response to Iago, who was the villain in the play.

Example: It was a foregone conclusion that he was going to lose in the election.

Fork in the road

Meaning: A point one of two possibilities has to be taken; A junction in which one road becomes two divergent roads.

Origin: This expression was likened to a road with several intersections. This could be used both literally and figuratively.

Example: Facing this fork in the road, it makes hard for me to decide on the next course of action.

Foul your own nest

Meaning: Do something damaging or harmful to yourself or your own interests.

Origin: This expression was likened to a bird who fouls or hurts its fledgling. This was then used figuratively to liken a person who abuses his family in the early 15th century.

Example: He fouled his own nest to win everybody's sympathy.

Founding father

Meaning: Someone who establishes an institution.

Origin: This expression was used to refer to the makers of the Federal Constitution Convention of 1787.

Example: John Smith is the founding father of our organization.

Freeze your blood

Meaning: Fill you with feelings of fear or horror.

Origin: In the Medieval era, blood was considered the hottest element of the body. If a person's blood froze because of horror, this would affect the proper function of supplying the body with heat and energy.

Example: She can easily freeze your blood with just a snap of her fingers.

Friendly fire

Meaning: Fire from one's own forces rather than enemy fire

Origin: This military expression was used during the Vietnam Conflict in the 1960s and was popularly used during the Gulf War of 1991.

Example: A friendly fire happened among the team members. Hopefully, they were able to resolve it.

Friends with benefits

Meaning: A sexual relationship with no long term commitment attached

Origin: This expression is one of the recent idioms in the 21st century. It was originally coined from a sitcom with the same title in 2011. But it was popularized in the movie starring Mila Kunis and Justin Timberlake in the same year.

Example: Mila and Justine were friends with benefits.

Frighten the horses

Meaning: Cause consternation or dismay; shock.

Origin: This expression was coined by English actress Mrs. Patrick Campbell. Campbell used this expression about male homosexual affairs when she quoted 'My dear, I don't care what they do, as long as they don't do it in the street and frighten the horses.'

Example: We may have frightened the horses with our loud actions.

From day one

Meaning: From the very start

Origin: This expression doesn't have a clear origin. However, it was cited in many printed references. One of them is in the 2013 New Zealand Herald with the topic of sudden deaths. It was written as "For sudden deaths like this ... they ought to go in with quite a suspicious mind from day one and treat it like a crime scene from the first moment."

Example: I know that she would do wonders from day one.

From head to toe (or foot)

Meaning: All over your body.

Origin: An alternative formulation with the same meaning is from top to toe.

Example: She glared at me from head to toe.

Fudge factor

Meaning: A figure which is included in a calculation in order to account for some unquantified but significant phenomenon or to ensure the desired result.

Origin: The word "fudge" was first used during the mid-18th century to express disgust and irritation. It was only in the later years that it was used as a printer's jargon which means 'do work imperfectly or as best you can with the materials available.

Example: What should we do for the fudge factor?

Full of beans

Meaning: Flamboyantly full of himself.

Origin: This expression's origin seems to be unclear. However, they believe that it stemmed from the practice of feeding beans to horses which makes them high-spirited.

Example: You are full of beans, I can't handle it.

Full to the gunwales

Meaning: Not enough space left

Origin: The gunwales or gun walls are on the top side of the ship above the gun port. When a sailor says it's full to the gunwales it means that the boat is literally full.

Example: My closet is full of gunwales.

Fun and games

Meaning: Amusing and enjoyable activities.

Origin: Refers to the activities that are more amusing to do.

Example: There was fun and games at the park.

Future shock

Meaning: A state of distress or disorientation due to rapid social or technological change.

Origin: This expression was first coined by American writer Alvin Toffler in his book titled "Horizon'. He defines it as 'the dizzying disorientation brought on by the premature arrival of the future.

Example: The older generation is easily future shocked because of the current technological and social trends.

G)

Game of cat and mouse

Meaning: The first person constantly deceives or baits the second person for them to take advantage of the situation.

Origin: This phrase was taken from the Indian Sanskrit tale of a lion, a cat, and a mouse which was attributed to Hitopadesha in 1675.

Example: In the game of cat and mouse, the smartest will always win.

Garbage in, garbage out

Meaning: Incorrect or poor quality input inevitably produces faulty output.

Origin: This expression is abbreviated as GIGO. It was first coined in the mid-20th century in the field of computing.

Example: Always remember, garbage in, garbage out. Conversions don't always make a bad picture.

Get a life

Meaning: To get your life together; to stop wasting your time on doing trivial things; ask a boring person to do something out of his comfort zone

Origin: The true origin of this expression is unknown. However, it was first recorded in the 20th century, printed in the Washington Post in 1983.

Example: John had told her to get a life. He doesn't want anything to do with her.

Get one's feet wet

Meaning: To begin taking part in a new activity; To try or experience something new or risky

Origin: This expression was traced back to Ancient Rome. This expression was taken from an anointing ritual for Caesar's Army where soldiers have to get their feet wet before they do something new in battle.

Example: It is time for Ciara to get her feet wet on her new business.

Get out of dodge

Meaning: To leave; To depart from the place with urgency

Origin: This expression dates back to the late 19th century in Dodge City, Kansas. Dodge City was known to be "a wicked little town". Aside from being a cattle town, Dodge City was known for its illegal pastimes like brothels, gambling dens, saloons and shootout areas.

Example: I think it's best that we get out of dodge before something happens again.

Get out of hand

Meaning: Out of control

Origin: This expression was likened to the idea of the horse getting out of control. Once the rider lets go of the reins, then he won't be able to control the horse.

Example: I want you to stay here before things get out of hand.

Get the lead out

Meaning: To move faster

Origin: This expression was first coined in the mid-20th century as jazz slang. It used to mean to 'play at a brisk speed.

Example: We need to get the lead out before anyone else does.

Get the sack

Meaning: Be fired from a job.

Origin: Originated in the 1500s when workers used to carry their belongings in a sack. Since they didn't have a locker area then, they used to put their sacks in their boss's office. Usually, they get their sacks after their shift or when their boss would fire them. Hence, the idiom 'give them their sack'.

Example: John has to get the sack because of his behavior.

Get under your skin

Meaning: Provoke or annoy someone; or have someone preoccupied.

Origin: The idea behind this phrase is very literal. It means that if you get under the first layer of your skin, it will cause irritation. However, this irritation doesn't cause any harm to you, but it will get you scratching and preoccupied.

Example: Some people can get under your skin.

Get underway

Meaning: Moving on the way

Origin: This expression was taken from the movement of the boat when it is moving through the water. These small bows in the water help the boat to move forward.

Example: The next step of the project should get underway.

Getting hitched

Meaning: Getting married

Origin: This refers to a rope that is made fast and stems during the 1760s. Most people also say that hitches also refer to making a high knot that keeps the ropes and sails in place.

Example: My eldest sister is finally getting hitched.

Ginger group

Meaning: A highly active faction within a party or movement that presses for stronger action on a particular issue.

Origin: Inspired by the practice of making broken-horses lively in the 18th century. Horse dealers would insert ginger into the anus of the horse to liven them up.

Example: The ginger group has been actively campaigning for their candidate.

Give a leg up

Meaning: Helping someone cross a hurdle

Origin: This expression was based on helping someone mount a horse by boosting their leg up.

Example: Give a leg up to people who have been having a hard time.

Give a wide berth

Meaning: Keep at a safe distance; avoid.

Origin: This idiom dated back to the 1600s. The berth is an area of the ship where it is moored at anchor, be it in the harbor or at sea. If the ship is at berth in the sea, it will float around the tide or wind but not too far from its anchor. However, if the ship is at berth in the harbor, the captain would give it a wide berth to avoid collisions in the dock. Hence the expression.

Example: We decided to give a wide berth to make it easier for people to pass through.

Give it a shot

Meaning: To make an attempt on something; or to try

Origin: There is no clear origin on how this expression came to be. However, the idea of "shot" is often used to mean an attempt of doing something.

Example: Let's give it a shot. We might be able to make it work.

Give someone their head

Meaning: Allow someone complete freedom of action.

Origin: This expression was taken from the idea of allowing a horse to go as fast without checking the pace between the bit and reins.

Example: I am going to give you your head and let's see how this project would go under your tutelage.

Gnash your teeth

Meaning: Feel or express anger or fury.

Origin: Gnashing of teeth while crying was often associated with anger and rage in the Bible. One of the examples of this expression is taken from Matthew 8:12: where it was written as 'But the children of the kingdom shall be cast out into outer darkness: there shall be weeping and gnashing of teeth.'

Example: He gnashed his teeth when he heard the news.

Go AWOL

Meaning: to take leave without permission (an acronym for absent without leave)

Origin: This expression was first used during the American Civil War. Soldiers who absented themselves in the roll call will bore the placard bearing the abbreviation AWOL. This soldier was not yet considered a deserter.

Example: She will have to go AWOL if they won't approve her leave.

Go ballistic

Meaning: Excessively enraged, irritated, and possibly violent.

Origin: This expression was inspired by controversy about ballistic missiles during the mid-1980s.

Example: Don't go ballistic when things don't go your way.

Go bananas

Meaning: Go crazy

Origin: This expression does not have a clear origin. However, some people believe that bananas have something to do with monkeys.

Example: Zac will go bananas when he sees his birthday present.

Go Dutch

Meaning: Each person pays for their own

Origin: It was inspired by a certain practice in Holland during the 17th century during the Anglo-Dutch Wars.

Example: We decided to go Dutch on the bill.

Go figure!

Meaning: Another expression for 'go now'

Origin: This expression comes from the Yiddish expression Gey vays, which literally means, 'go now.' It was then used colloquially during the late 1970s to early 80s.

Example: Go figure! You don't realize how much time you just have wasted talking.

Go gangbusters

Meaning: Proceed very vigorously or successfully.

Origin: The word "gangbuster" is defined as "the person who breaks up or catches violent criminal gangs". Most of the time, gangbusters are often police officers or other influential people.

Example: We should go gangbusters for this project.

Go off the deep end

Meaning: To become irrational and to act with your emotions and not with your head.

Origin: This expression was taken from the idea of someone who doesn't know how to swim deciding to jump into the deepest end of the swimming pool.

Example: You don't need to go off the deep end. You need to think with your head and not your emotions.

Go out on a limb

Meaning: Get into a position where others do not support you; Take a wild guess

Origin: This expression was an allusion to climbing trees and going out a branch. The biggest risk of standing on a branch is that the branch may not be sturdy enough to hold your weight.

Example: They told the group to go out on a limb and surprise them with another amazing act.

Go the extra mile

Meaning: Be especially assiduous in your attempt to achieve something.

Origin: This expression was cited in the New Testament in the Book of Matthew 5:41 where it was written as "And whosoever shall compel thee to go a mile, go with him twain"

Example: There is nothing wrong with going the extra mile for our loved ones.

Go the whole nine yards

Meaning: To give your all toward something.

Origin: This idiom originated during World War II. Every plane pilot has a set of ammunition with a length of 9 yards. These pilots promised to give their all during the war, Hence, the expression "go the whole nine yards."

Example: I am going to go the whole nine yards for this project.

Go through fire (and water)

Meaning: Face any peril.

Origin: This expression was taken from a Medieval practice of trial by order wherein the suspect should hold or walk on a red-hot iron or be thrown into the water.

Example: My dog will go through fire and water to ensure our safety.

Go with the flow

Meaning: Follow along with the situation and accept what is currently going on.

Origin: This expression was first inspired by the tides and currents of the ocean. It describes boats or things that are floating in the flow of the sea.

Example: Just go with the flow. I know this plan will work.

Good Samaritan

Meaning: A charitable or helpful person.

Origin: This idiomatic expression was taken from the parable of a Man who went from Jerusalem to Jericho. In Luke 10, this injured man was ignored by the people of the same status and belief but was helped by someone who was of a different belief.

Example: Peter is a Good Samaritan. He has a good heart.

Graveyard shift

Meaning: Night shift

Origin: This expression was taken from the idea of "ghostlike hour" which refers to late night working schedules.

Example: I don't like being on the graveyard shift.

Great white hope

Meaning: Someone or something expected to achieve great success

Origin: The Great White Hope has its origins traced back to the sporting arena. This idiomatic expression comes with a negative connotation behind it. In 1908, the first black African American boxer, Jack Jackson, became the first black man to beat the Canadian Boxer, Tommy Burns, in Sydney, Australia Due to racial animosity, retired white American Boxer James Jeffries came out from retirement to fight against Johnson. Jeffries was then called the Great White Hope. However, Jeffries was beaten by Johnson during their bout.

Example: Marie was her family's Great White Hope. They knew she was going to be successful someday.

Green light

Meaning: Permission to go ahead with a project.

Origin: This expression refers to the traffic system that was invented in the 19th century. Red means stop and green means go.

Example: The management has given me the green light to work on the new assignment.

Green thumb

Meaning: Someone good at gardening

Origin: This expression was first used in the UK in the early 1900s. It was believed that this expression came to be from the green stains on the farmers and crop growers, after planting crops all day.

Example: Marigold has a green thumb! Look at how her garden thrives.

Green-eyed monster

Meaning: Jealous

Origin: Green was often associated with sickness. However, it was only during the time of Shakespeare that the word "green-eyed monster" was used to signify jealousy. In his play Merchant of Venice, he used the words "green with envy."

Example: The green-eyed monster was not happy with the interaction.

Grin and bear it

Meaning: Suffer pain or misfortune in a stoical manner.

Origin: This expression was first coined in the mid-17th century when it was meant to mean an act of showing their teeth or a snarl which was very derogatory. However, it was only in the 19th century that this expression was used to mean "suffer pain or misfortune in a stoical manner."

Example: We must grin and bear it for now so that we can leave the meeting unscathed.

Guiding light

Meaning: Someone who plays an important influence on your life

Origin: This expression was likened to the idea of a flashlight that illuminates a person's path when it's dark. The origin of this expression remains unknown but it has been one of the most commonly used idioms in the present times.

Expression: Mother Teresa is the guiding light of many nuns in the world.

Gut feeling

Meaning: Intuition, Instinctive feeling

Origin: This expression comes from a certain belief that emotions come from our stomach area. They call this area the gut.

Example: I have a gut feeling this won't end very well.

Hair of the dog

Meaning: A small quantity of alcohol taken as a remedy for a hangover.

Origin: This expression was taken from the proverb "hair of the dog that bit you". In the past. It was believed that the hair of rabid dogs used to be a remedy for dog bites. Aside from that, it was also suggested as a remedy for hangovers.

Example: One way of getting over a hangover is drinking another hair of the dog.

Half a loaf

Meaning: Not as much as you want but better than nothing.

Origin: This phrase shows an allusion to the proverb which is "half a loaf is better than no bread" which has been used since the mid 16th century

Example: Half a loaf is better than none.

Hand over fist

Meaning: Quickly; at a fast rate.

Origin: Currently, this expression is usually related to making fast money. However, its first usage was during the 1700s. Instead of "hand over fist", it was originally "hand over hand". This expression was used to describe a sailor on how fast he climbed up or haul the rope. After the years passed, this expression was later modified to hand over fist, which described the flat hand passing over the clenched fist on the rope.

Example: The business is lucrative. They have been making profits hand over fist.

Hands are tied

Meaning: Nothing you can do to change the situation. The state of being helpless.

Origin: This expression was taken from modern day situations that we cannot change or fix.This expression was believed to be coined in the 18th century, where it was associated with the idea of your hands being tied literally.

Example: I'm sorry, Kim, my hands are tied and there is nothing we can do about it.

Hang out to dry

Meaning: Abandoned or left hanging or suspended

Origin: This expression was taken from the idea of air drying your clothes on the clothesline.

Example: She left me hanging out to dry in a place I don't even know.

Hang tight

Meaning: To remain in the same position.

Origin: Hang tight is an expression that comes from holding the ropes that control the jib boom. This way, they are able to navigate away from their enemies or change location away from troubled waters.

Example: Don't give up! Just hang tight, ok?

Hang up your boots

Meaning: Stop working; retire.

Origin: Boots are a part of a person's work attire. This is also synonymous with the Canadian expression "hang up your skates."

Example: After several injuries, Mark decided to hang up his boots despite his young age.

Hanging by a thread

Meaning: Ready to fall apart

Origin: This expression was taken from a classic Greek Legend where King Dionysius has threatened one of his courtiers, Damascoles. He threatened him by making him sit beneath a sword that was hanging by the single hair of a horse's tail.

Example: My patience is hanging by a thread.

Happy as a sandboy

Meaning: Extremely happy; perfectly content with your situation.

Origin: The word sandboy was used to refer to an urchin who sold sand in the street based on the 1823 dictionary. The word sandboy was also defined as 'a merry fellow who has tasted a drop'.

Example: Mike was as happy as a sandboy when he saw his best friend after 20 years.

Happy go lucky

Meaning: Cheerful; accepts life as it comes; goes with the flow

Origin: This expression was first coined in the 1670s. However, this expression doesn't really mean the way we know it. The word "hap" was taken from the Old Norse word "happ" which means good fortune However, the definition changed throughout the years.

Example: You shouldn't be so happy-go-lucky with all the things happening right now.

Hard and fast

Meaning: Rigidly adhered to; inflexible

Origin: This idiom originated from a certain situation at sea. When a ship was grounded on land, they are considered hard and fast. They are not able to move it until a strong tide comes in.

Example: It came in hard and fast, we didn't know how to react.

Harp on

Meaning: To speak on continuously about things that are not interesting; talk in boring tone

Origin: This expression was coined during the 1600s. It refers to the music that a harp makes. Harps can be soothing to the ears and make you sleep. However, the definition of the expression started to change into being boring.

Example: She continued to harp on about the beauty of art to people who don't really find it interesting.

Haul someone over the coals

Meaning: To give someone a severe reprimand

Origin: Taken from a ritual to test a person's innocence. In the mid 15th to 16th century, suspects were hauled over a bed of glowing coals. If the suspect survived, he was considered innocent. But if the suspect died, then he was guilty of the charge.

Example: My boss hauled me over the coals for my mistake at work.

Have an ace up your sleeve

Meaning: Have an effective resource or piece of information kept hidden until it is necessary to use it; have a secret advantage.

Origin: This idiom was created from the idea that the ace is the biggest high playing card. In casinos, it was always depicted that a cheating player would often have an ace card up his sleeve and would swap it out unnoticed.

Example: You must have an ace up your sleeve if you are willing to bet this much.

Have front row seats to

Meaning: Someone is in an excellent position to have knowledge of important information.

Origin: This expression was first cited in the article Russia on our Minds: Reflections on another World, 1970, by Delilah and Ferdinand Kuhn: "And we, as reporters on foreign assignments, happened to have front-row seats to watch the Russians in a brand-new role."

Example: The secretary has front row seats to the meeting that is currently taking place.

Have one's heart set on something

Meaning: To want something so much that obtaining it becomes a person's focus

Origin: This expression was taken from the late 14th century. English poet George Chaucer used it in the book of Troilus and Criseyde in 1385. He wrote, "Why not love another sweet lady, who may set your heart at ease?"

Example: Once you have your heart set on something, you are going to give it your all just to achieve it.

Have someone in one's pocket

Meaning: Having control over someone

Origin: It was first used in 1931 when it appeared in Francis Henry Gribble's Emperor and Mystic. The Life of Alexander I of Russia. He wrote, "Some of his colleagues — notably those Prussians who called him 'their Alexander' and believed that they had him in their pocket — were playing an undisguised game of grab, and wanted to annex territory without the least regard for any..."

Example: Jeremy won't come if you don't ask Alice first. She has him in her pocket.

Have something sewed up

Meaning: Have control over something to gain favorable results in the future.

Origin: The first citation was taken from The Life and Opinions of Tristram Shadny, Gentleman by Laurence Sterne. He wrote "The nymphs joined in unison, and their swains an octave below them. I would have given a crown to have had it sewed up. — Nannette would not have given a sous, — Viva la joia was in her lips..."

Example: Mr. Whitey has everything sewed up for Jenny's future.

Have the bit between your teeth

Meaning: Take control of a situation

Origin: This expression was taken from horse racing. The word "bit" was taken from the Old English word meaning "bite". The bit was the mouthpiece in a horse's bridle which was used to control the horse's movement.

Example: Captain James has the bit between his teeth. The Mary Weather will be able to pass through the storm.

Have the last laugh

Meaning: Be finally vindicated, thereby confounding earlier skepticism.

Origin: This expression was taken from the proverb "He laughs best, who laughs last and he who laughs last, laughs longest."

Example: Let's see who will have the last laugh.

Head in the clouds

Meaning: Used to describe someone who is not being realistic.

Origins: This idiom has been around since the mid-1600s. The origins of this expression are unclear beyond the obvious imagery of someone who is a bit of a fantasist (having one's head in the clouds is clearly impossible – or at least it was in the days before aviation!).

Example: She has her head in the clouds after meeting her idol today.

Head on a platter

Meaning: The desire to punish someone out of anger.

Origin: This expression was taken from the Bible. John the Baptist was beheaded by King Herod because of a hideous wish from his mistress, Salome, who had asked for John the Baptist's head on a platter.

Example: He wanted her head on a platter after she betrayed his trust.

Heads are gonna roll

Meaning: Employees are going to be fired over some specific infraction, misjudgment, or incident

Origin: This expression was first used in the middle to late 20th century. It was first used as a reference in The Kenyon Review, Kenyon College, Volume 31, 1969: "...one slat offense in this district without Mason's picture on it by tomorrow morning, well, some heads are gonna roll around here."

Example: I can see heads are gonna roll if you don't start working.

Heads up

Meaning: Warn someone ahead of time

Origin: This expression was taken from the fact that a head up is a task required by someone to look at something that is a non-issue. It would also prepare them for possible future opportunities.

Example: Give me a heads up if you are coming to visit.

Hedge your bets

Meaning: Try to minimize the risk of being wrong or incurring loss by pursuing two courses of action at the same time.

Origin: This expression is inspired by the idea of Hedging. Hedging is a way or a method to help one minimize one's financial liabilities.

Example: We all need to hedge our bets if we don't want to end up losing money in the end.

Hell bent for leather

Meaning: To go all out, willing to do anything to achieve a goal

Origin: This expression was originally from horse riding. The word bent means "to be determined". With this in mind, these horse riders would often be forced to ride their horse to their hardest until their horses were injured and incapable. Because of this, horses were considered useless and their skins were turned into leather. That's how the expression was coined.

Example: She was hell-bent on leather to get that big teddy bear in the carnival.

High jinks

Meaning: Excited and silly behavior when people are enjoying themselves.

Origin: This word is originally from a popular drinking game in Scotland in the 1700s. High Jinks is a game where the dice are thrown and the players can make a score out of the dice. The loser with the smallest score would then take the most potent cocktail of alcohol that can make you drunk and foolish.

Example: We all got high jinks after seeing Dawson dancing on the dance floor.

High, wide, and handsome

Meaning: Expansive and impressive; stylish and carefree in manner.

Origin: This expression was originally from the US and it is also known as Yankee Slang. People would often refer to it as "Ride him, Cowboy, high, wide, and handsome."

Example: He is one of the actors that I consider high, wide, and handsome.

Hit the jackpot

Meaning: Win a jackpot. Have great or unexpected success, especially in making a lot of money quickly.

Origin: This expression was taken from a game of poker. The word jackpot refers to the pot that every player has added to before the game.

Example: Looks like we hit the jackpot with this lot.

Hit the mark

Meaning: Be successful in an attempt or accurate in a guess.

Origin: The word "mark" referred to here is a target in shooting.

Example: You hit the mark on that question.

Hit the nail on the head

Meaning: Correct; precise

Origin: First cited in a printed citation of The Book of Margery Kempe, about 1438. In proper English, it was quoted as "If I hear any more of these matters repeated, I shall so smite (hit) the nail on the head that it shall shame all her supporters."

Example: All the answers hit the nail on the head!

Hit the panic button

Meaning: Prepare for disaster; react badly on the situation

Origin: This expression was taken from an actual panic button in aircraft. This switch is used to jettison things that make the plane heavy.

Example: I hit the panic button when I saw him pass me by.

Hit the road

Meaning: Depart; Set out on a trip

Origin: This phrase was inspired by the pounding of the horses' hooves as soon as they departed from the place. It also refers to car tires or your feet when you are leaving your current area for another. This expression was first cited in 1873 with a similar expression by W.F Butler called "hit the trail"

Example: It's time that we hit the road. The earlier we leave, the faster we arrive at our destination.

Hit the roof

Meaning: Lose your temper or become enraged/infuriated.

Origin: This idiom was first used in the 19th century." It gives an allusion to getting angry to the point of banging your head on the roof or ceiling of the house. It was likened to the idea of exploding.

Example: I didn't expect him to hit the roof after losing in the game six times in a row.

Hold the gun to someone's head

Meaning: Exerting extreme pressure on someone

Origin: First cited in the printed reference of the book Critical Teaching and Everyday Life by Ira Shor, originally published in Canada in 1945. It was written as "After all, no one forced you to go to college; no one held a gun to your head."

Example: He was holding a gun to her head, telling her to tell them the truth.

Hold the line

Meaning: Not to surrender in whatever situation; maintain a telephone connection during a break in the conversation.

Origin: This military expression was used to refer to the idea of a line of soldiers defending and attacking the enemy without moving from their position.

Example: When this gets tough, just hold the line. Everything will be alright.

Hold tongue

Meaning: To keep quiet and not to say anything.

Origin: This expression is a synonym to the expression "bite your tongue". It refers to the idea that one should hold their tongue to refrain from saying anything. This expression was often used as part of the traditional wedding vows when the officiant would say "Speak now or forever hold your peace."

Example: If I were you, I'd hold my tongue and not say anything.

Hold your horses

Meaning: Wait; hold

Origin: This expression was discovered in the 19th century. It was inspired by the idea of pulling the reins of the horses to stop them from running.

Example: Hold your horses, we don't even know if it's a boy or a girl!

Horses for courses

Meaning: Different people are suited to different things or situations.

Origin: This phrase was first recorded in A. E. T. Watson's Turf (1891) which was written as 'A familiar phrase on the turf is "horses for courses"...the Brighton Course is very like Epsom, and horses that win at one meeting often win at the other'.

Example: We all have our horses for courses.

Hot chase

Meaning: Chase

Origin: This expression is similar to hot pursuit. Hot chase and hot pursuit allow ships to chase possible trespassers that enter their territorial waters. In current times, this expression is also a doctrine used by many law officers when pursuing a criminal.

Example: Authorities are in the middle of a hot chase with a criminal on the road.

I could (couldn't) care less

Meaning: Not interested in the topic

Origin: This British expression was first used in 1946 in the book by Anthony Phelps with the same title. It was inspired by his experiences in the Air Transport Auxiliary during World War II. This expression became popular as soon as it reached the American shores in 1950.

Example: I couldn't care less if you go to the party or not.

I could eat a horse

Meaning: Extremely hungry

Origin: The origin of this idiom remains unknown. However, if you think about it, a horse is a large animal." Perhaps, it was used to exaggerate the idea of eating a huge amount of food.

Example: I am so hungry that I could eat a horse.

I've got it in the bag

Meaning: Secured success

Origin: It was inspired from a superstition that was popularized by the New York Giants. The team would often carry a bag with 72 balls and spread these balls in the playing field. Players would use these balls when the other balls were no longer fit for use and were too dirty. This superstition became the reason for the Giants having a 26-game winning streak.

Example: Don't worry, I've got it in the bag! We will win this.

Icing on the cake

Meaning: Extra feature, something that makes the situation a lot even better.

Origin: This expression was first referred to the icing that makes the cake a cake even better This expression can be both used in a positive and negative, depending on the connotation. In the past, people used to enjoy cake without the frosting. With the added icing, it made the cake a lot more special.

Example: Her presence was the biggest icing on the cake of John's birthday.

In (or into) the groove

Meaning: Performing well or confidently, especially in an established pattern; indulging in relaxed and spontaneous enjoyment, especially dancing

Origin: The word groove is a spiral track cut in a gramophone that was recorded in the path of the needle. However, the expression continually changed in the 20th century. Groove was then taken to the context of jazz music.

Example: This dancer is the groove! See how many people he has captivated with his dancing.

In a cleft stick

Meaning: In a predicament, unable to decide which way to go

Origin: This expression alludes to the idea of trapping a snake by using a forked stick behind its head.

Example: I'm in a cleft stick. I can't choose.

In a nutshell

Meaning: In conclusion; to sum it up briefly

Origin: This figurative expression was used in the book In Curiosities of Literature, by Isaac Disraeli. He used this expression to summarize The Iliad by Homer

Example: In a nutshell, the story of the Titanic didn't end up really well.

In a pickle

Meaning: In a difficult situation, in a mess

Origin: This phrase was derived from the idea of pickling vegetables and meat during the Middle Ages. Because of the long hard winter, people then had to pickle their food to preserve it throughout the winter. Fresh food is often scarce during the winter season.

Example: We were all stuck in a pickle because the children were left unattended before the event.

In apple-pie order

Meaning: With everything neatly arranged, in its proper place

Origin: This expression comes with different origins. However, it was believed that it was taken from the Old French cap, a pie which was translated to 'clothed in armor from head to foot' which referred to the soldier's complete and proper outfit for war.

Example: Make sure that everything is in apple-pie order.

In broad daylight

Meaning: During the daytime; Used to express when something unconventional is done openly

Origin: This expression was first cited in 1579. However, there is no clear idea when this expression came to be. It was often used to depict unconventional events happening in the mornings. For example, "robbed in broad daylight."

Example: The DUI accident happened in broad daylight.

In deep water (or waters)

Meaning: In trouble or difficulty.

Origin: This biblical idiom was taken from Psalm 69:14 where it was written as 'let me be delivered from them that hate me, and out of the deep waters.'

Example: We will be in deep waters if we don't do something about this.

In harness

Meaning: In the routine of daily work; Working closely with someone to achieve something.

Origin: This expression was likened to a horse or animal that are often used in farming.

Example: They are working in harness to ensure that they are able to track the progress of this project.

In hot water

Meaning: In trouble or state of shame

Origin: Dating back to the 1600s, this expression shows an allusion to being in hot water. Another origin story of this expression was taken to ancient times. People would throw a cauldron filled with hot water at their intruders.

Example: We were in hot water for sometime because of the riot we caused.

In sackcloth and ashes

Meaning: Manifesting grief or repentance.

Origin: This idiom originated in the Bible. It was said that the wearing of a sackcloth and the sprinkling of ashes on your head were signs of penitence or mourning.

Example: We were all sackcloths and ashes after our grandmother's death.

In seventh heaven

Meaning: In ecstasy, in sheer delight

Origin: It was taken from the Muslim belief of the seven heavens which corresponds to the seven planets. It is believed that the Most High sits in the 7th heaven where it is covered in precious gems and gold. Another possible origin of this idiom is taken from the idea that 7 is also a perfect and lucky number.

Example: I am floating in seventh heaven after tasting her chocolate cake.

In stitches

Meaning: Laughing so hard that your sides hurt.

Origins: Presumably comparing the physical pain of intense laughter with the prick of a needle. But the expression "in stitches" was first used in 1602 by Shakespeare in Twelfth Night. After that, the expression wasn't recorded again until the 20th century, but it's now commonplace.

Example: I was left in stitches after hearing her joke.

In tandem

Meaning: One behind another; alongside each other; together.

Origin: This expression was originally from the Latin word tandem means 'at length': This two expression was a term used to refer to a carriage drawn by two horses. But as the years passed, the expression evolved and was referred to as 'functioning as a team.

Example: I saw guys riding in tandem. It seems like they were going on a road trip.

In the buff

Meaning: Naked

Origin: This expression was inspired from a buff-coat. This coat is a light leather tunic worn by English soldiers in the 17th century. The expression in the buff used to mean wearing the buff coat. However, because of its similar color to the human flesh, it was then used to refer to nudity.

Example: Many people are in the buff during the hot summer weather.

In the doldrums

Meaning: To feel unmotivated or depressed.

Origin: "In the doldrums" is a region located slightly north of the equator in between two belts of winds. The winds would often meet around this belt where they try to neutralize each other. Because of this, many ships were left stranded and unable to sail. Although many people thought the expression was coined because of the region, it was because of the nature of the region. In Old English, Doldrum comes from the word "dol" which means "dull". Currently, Doldrum is now known as the Intertropical Convergence Zone. However, this expression has been used figuratively since the 19th century.

Example: I have been in the doldrums for the past few weeks.

In the grand scheme of things

Meaning: Something that is not important compared to the entire scope of everything.

Origin: This expression was cited in the early 20th century. Although there was no clear evidence of its origin, it was first used in many printed references. In the article ' An American System of Economics' by C.A. Bowsher in Moody's Magazine wrote "Land, gold and collective man are derivative relations in the grand scheme of things when contrasted with value."

Example: In the grand scheme of things, this information doesn't really matter at all.

In the loop

Meaning: To be aware or included, up to date with the situation

Origin: This expression was taken from military officials where they command people to be in the feedback loop. This way, every personnel in the military is aware of the situation.

Example: Please keep me in the loop of the current situation at home.

In the nick of time

Meaning: Last minute

Origin: This expression was first inspired by tallies or nick-stick to keep records of score in the past. This expression is related to the expression "to nick it down" or to record it down. In the nick, time was referred to as the last point to be recorded before the time is up.

Example: I was able to submit my assignment in the nick of time.

In the offing

Meaning: Likely to happen soon; imminent

Origin: This expression was first dated from the 1600s but was only used from the late 1700s. The phrase "in the offing" referred to the visible part between the shore and the horizon. The ship would be "in the offing" when they can see this visible part. The lookout would shout and tell the captain that they are in the offing to prepare the ship for docking.

Example: Waiting for the project to be in the offing.

In the pipeline

Meaning: On the way, about to happen, about to be implemented

Origin: This expression was taken from oil traders and how the system piping was installed during the 1880s. It carries oil from the well to the refinery with the use of a pipeline.

Example: There are many projects in the pipeline.

In the red

Meaning: In debt

Origin: This idiom was taken from the field of bookkeeping. The entries that are considered a "loss" are written in red ink while the entries that add profit or any positive amount in the ledger are written in black.

Example: They were in the red since last year.

In the wings

Meaning: Ready to do something or to be used at the appropriate time.

Origin: This idiom comes from the theater, in which the wings are the areas screened from public view where actors wait for their cue to come on stage.

Example: She was in the wings for the next theater auditions.

In this day and age

Meaning: At this present time

Origin: It was cited in a 2003 movie called Inside Out. It was cited as "The idea of girls becoming a commodity, to be traded as slaves, seems totally alien in this day and age."

Example: In this day and age, women have been able to fight for their rights.

In your face

Meaning: Bold and defiant move.

Origin: This expression was coined during the 1970s in the US. It was often used as a sports idiom during confrontation. It was only in the 1980s that people used this expression figuratively.

Example: As soon the door opens, then it is that reality hits you in your face.

Indian summer

Meaning: A period of dry, warm weather occurring in late autumn. A tranquil or productive period in someone's later years.

Origin: This expression was first used in the US. it alludes to the warm autumn season in the areas where Native Americans resided.

Example: It's autumn but yet here we are with our coats off because of the Indian Summer.

Iron out the wrinkles

Meaning: Resolve all minor difficulties and snags.

Origin: This expression was taken from the idea of ironing clothes. It was first used in the mid-19th century.

Example: As soon as we iron out the wrinkles, we can proceed with confidence.

It isn't over till the fat lady sings

Meaning: There is still time for a situation to change.

Origin: This expression was taken from the saying "The opera isn't over till the fat lady sings" in the 1970s.

Example: The game isn't over till the fat lady sings!

It takes one to know one

Meaning: A derogatory expression used to express the idea that a person with the similar traits would recognize another

Origin: It was cited in 1927 in the English version of the French political publication Les Réalités. It was cited as "His cartoons hit home and drew blood from politics, business, religion, justice, the theater. Apparently, it takes one to know one."

Example: It takes a villain to know another villain.

It takes two to tango

Meaning: People involved in the situation are both responsible for the situation

Origin: The expression originated and was made popular in 1952. It was written by Al Hoffman and Dick Manning in a book with the same title. This expression meant that both sides should work together to make things work.

Example: It takes two to tango when it comes to having a peaceful relationship.

It's all Greek to me

Meaning: Can't understand at all

Origin: This expression was coined by Shakespeare in his famous play "Julius Caesar". It was taken from the part where Cicero used the Greek language to avoid Roman passersby and Casca to understand what he was saying.

Example: Everything was all Greek to me until she taught me how to use the computer.

It's like apples and oranges

Meaning: Two incomparable things.

Origin: There is no clear origin on how this expression started but it used to be apples and oysters before it was changed to apples and oranges. This expression was possibly coined by John Ray in 1670.

Example: Jin and Mara are like apples and oranges. You can't compare people with different perspectives.

Chapter "Good Will"

Helping others without expectation of anything in return has been proven to lead to increased happiness and satisfaction in life.

We would love to give you the chance to experience that same feeling during your reading experience today...

All it takes is a few moments of your time to answer one simple question:

Would you make a difference in the life of someone you've never met—without spending any money or seeking recognition for your good will?

If so, we have a small request for you.

If you've found value in your reading experience today, we humbly ask that you take a brief moment right now to leave an honest review of this book. It won't cost you anything but 30 seconds of your time—just a few seconds to share your thoughts with others.

Your voice can go a long way in helping someone else find the

same inspiration and knowledge that you have.

Scan the QR code below:

OR

Visit the link below:

https://geni.us/b3SxCl

Thank you in advance!

J)

Jekyll and Hyde

Meaning: A person alternately displaying opposing good and evil personalities.

Origin: This expression was inspired by the novel "The Strange Case of Dr. Jekyll and Mr. Hyde" by Robert Louis Stevenson. It talks about Dr. Jekyll who wanted to indulge his evil instincts. He created a drug to create the persona of Mr. Hyde who gradually gained total control over his body.

Example: We all have our own version of Jekyll and Hyde in ourselves.

Join the club!

Meaning: A common unfortunate experience

Origin: The origin of this expression is unknown. However, it was first used in the UK during the late 1940s.

Example: Join the club! I was a victim of the same situation the other day.

Joined at the hip

Meaning: Inseparable in opinions or outlook.

Origin: The metaphor is based on the idea of literal conjoined twins.

Example: Elle and Dakota are really close, they are practically joined at the hip.

Jump the gun

Meaning: To begin a project before the necessary preparations have been made

Origin: This expression was inspired by the expression "Beat the gun" which was originally from track and field. It was inspired by the firing of the starting pistol.

Example: Don't jump the gun if you are not fully prepared.

Jump the shark

Meaning: The moment when a form of entertainment reaches a decline in quality by including gimmicks to maintain interest.

Origin: This expression was inspired by the show Happy Days where a character literally jumps over a shark while water skiing.

Example: She made us jump the shark!

Jump through hoops

Meaning: Overcoming the obstacles in order to accomplish the goals

Origin: This expression was first cited in the early 19th century. It was used to describe circus animals jumping through hoops by their trainers.

Example: She jumped through the hoops and made all her dreams come true.

Jump to conclusions

Meaning: To make (a foolish) decision before knowing it thoroughly; To predict a situation without having sufficient information

Origin: This expression was first cited in the early 1700s. However, many people don't really know its exact origin.

Example: Please don't jump to conclusions if you don't know the whole story.

Just what the doctor ordered

Meaning: Exactly what you are told

Origin: This expression was first used in 1930. It was from an early printed reference in the book called From a Colonial Governor's Notebook, A History of the Caribbean and West Indies by Sir Reginald St. Johnson. It was written as "And the captain, who was thirsty, said: 'That's just what the doctor ordered,' and heroically tossed it down at a gulp, while the rest of us took a preliminary sip in order to get the full benefit of the new flavour."

Example: Stop moving and drink just like what the doctor ordered.

K)

Kangaroo court

Meaning: Refers to a bogus or fake court.

Origin: This expression was taken from the claim jumping during the time of the California Gold Rush. This expression was first used in printed form in the magazine article by Philip Paxton which was titled A Stray Yankee in Texas. This article comes with the notion of Kangaroos jumping providing blank stares from people who saw them for the first time which is similar to the faces of the judges in Kangaroo Court.

Example: The current judges of this show are from a Kangaroo court.

Keeled over

Meaning: Suddenly fell down

Origin: Taken from the idea of the boat's keel sticking out of the water when the boat is upside down."

Example: Dane keeled over after jumping off the table.

Keep a stiff upper lip

Meaning: A steady and determined attitude or manner in the face of trouble

Origin: The expression first came in 1935. The British Empire had the feeling that one should do their duty without showing their emotions. This expression became popular in the US after its first printed reference was published in the form of a novel of the same title.

Example: She kept a stiff upper lip when she faced her rival.

Keep up with the Joneses

Meaning: Try to maintain the same social and material standards as your friends or neighbors.

Origin: This expression was inspired by the comic strip titled 'Keeping up with the Joneses—by Pop' The family name "Jones" is considered to be a common family name in the US. Hence it was used as a generic name for neighbors or presumed social equals.

Example: I need to keep up with the Joneses, especially in my new neighborhood.

Keep your nose clean

Meaning: Keeping away from undesirable influences that can harm your reputation

Origin: This expression was first cited in the article The Globe in Kansas City, Kansas, in May 1881. It was stated as "Mr. Lowell commenced railroading about sixteen years ago, as superintendent's private secretary, and by keeping his nose clean, brushing his clothes, and attending Sunday school regularly, he has succeeded…"

Example: Keep your nose clean and stop making friends with shady characters.

Keep your powder dry

Meaning: To save your resources until they are needed to avoid possible shortages

Origin: This expression was taken from the 19th century. This was used in Oliver Cromwell's campaign in Ireland. While they were crossing the river towards the enemy frontlines, Cromwell told his men that they should not waste their gunpowder which was already scarce. He said 'Put your faith in God and keep your powder dry. The wet gunpowder can lead them to a certain defeat.'

Example: Keep your powder dry, especially during the typhoon season.

Kick against the pricks

Meaning: Hurt yourself by persisting in useless resistance or protest.

Origin: It was taken from the Bible. On his way to Damascus, Saul heard a voice saying 'It is hard for thee to kick against the pricks.' (Acts 9:5). This expression was also likened to an ox or another beast fruitlessly kicking out when it is pricked.

Example: There will always be people who will kick against the pricks, especially if they know what they are fighting for is correct.

Kick the bucket

Meaning: To die.

Origin: This idiom used to be a slaughterhouse practice during the 16th century. Butchers would hang animals on a slaughter beam called a bucket. Animals that were killed on the bucket would usually convulse profusely; hence the idiom "kick the bucket"

Example: My dog kicked the bucket last night. He was 14 years old.

Kill someone with (or by) kindness

Meaning: Spoil someone by overindulging them.

Origin: This expression was first coined in the mid-16th century. It was the title of Thomas Heywood's play called "A Woman Killed with Kindness."

Example: Your sweet gesture is like killing me with kindness.

Kill two birds with one stone

Meaning: taking care of two things with one single effort.

Origin: There were similar phrases that were associated with this phrase. However, it was first cited in the 16th century in Thomas Hobbes's A Work on Liberty. He wrote "T. H. thinks to kill two birds with one stone and satisfy two arguments with one answer."

Example: Nara killed two birds with one stone by recycling this old mattress.

King of the castle

Meaning: Someone holding a pre-eminent position, rank, or place; a dominant or successful person.

Origin: This expression was taken from the game with the same title. A child would stand on a mound and say 'I'm the king of the castle. Get down, you dirty rascal!'. The other children would dare to pull him off the mound to become the next king of the castle.

Example: In the editing department, the editor-in-chief is the king of the castle.

Kiss of death

Meaning: An event that will cause the failure of an enterprise

Origin: This expression has a different origin. One of them is the kiss that Judas gave Jesus after he betrayed him. However, this expression was only then used by the American Mafia. The "kiss of death" is often given by the don to the person who has betrayed him.

Example: Her carelessness was the kiss of death that had led to her bankruptcy.

Kiss the rod

Meaning: Accept punishment meekly or submissively.

Origin: This expression was taken from a former practice of punishment for children. The child would kiss the rod before the child is beaten. It was also cited by Shakespeare in his work "Two Gentlemen of Verona" where he wrote, "How wayward is this foolish love That, like a testy babe, will scratch the nurse And presently all humbled kiss the rod."

Example: They kiss the rod because they know they did something wrong.

Knight in shining armor

Meaning: A knight in shining armor is a heroic, idealized male who typically comes to the rescue of a female.

Origins: The idiom was inspired from the days of Old England. Around this time chivalry and knights used to come and rescue damsels in distress. The earliest use of the expression was in a poem by Henry Pye in 1790, which referred to "No more the knight, in shining armour dress'd".

Example: His character reminds me of a knight in shining armor.

Knock it out of the park

Meaning: Doing a great job

Origin: This expression was inspired by hitting a home run when the baseball goes out of the ballpark. It had been used figuratively even up to now.

Example: Knock it out of the park! That was an amazing shot.

Knock the spots off

Meaning: To beat easily; to outdo completely.

Origin: This expression was first used in the mid-1800s. Carnivals were common places for entertainment. One of the most popular games in the past was shooting games. Many people tried to show their marksmanship skills. In the past, they used cards, the face of which had spots or marks indicating their value. The object was to shoot through all the spots and remove as many as possible. If anyone knocked off all the marks, they won the prize.

Example: Desmond knocked the spots off after playing his original composition on stage.

Knotty problem

Meaning: A complicated problem that is too difficult to solve.

Origin: The origin of this expression is currently unknown. However, it was believed to be likened to the ``knotty" part of the branches of a tree. These branches are left unpruned for a longer period of time. Because of this, it created complicated knots and made it a lot harder to cut.

Example: I think we need help to solve this knotty problem.

Know the ropes

Meaning: Well versed in something

Origin: This idiomatic expression was coined from the early sailing vessels in the 1600s. During this time, sails were controlled by different ropes and knots which are connected to the sails. The sailors were tasked to learn how to raise, lower, and maneuver the sails and the ship. Learning the ropes was a very difficult task for many sailors then. When they claimed that they had learned the ropes, it meant that they were well-versed in the intricate knots and ropes of the ship. It was only in the 1800s that this phrase was used figuratively.

Example: You need to know the ropes to understand the whole process.

Knuckle down

Meaning: To diligently apply oneself.

Origin: This idiom originated in the game of marbles. A marble, also known as a taw, is held with a crooked index finger and flicked by the thumb. One rule that you should always remember when playing marbles is that the knuckle of the index finger should be placed down on the ground before taking a shot. It should also be in the exact position of the player's previous marble. If the player does not follow the rule will be told to concentrate and knuckle down.

Example: We all need to knuckle down to get the healthy condition we are aiming for.

Larger than life

Meaning: A flamboyant, gregarious person whose mannerisms or appearance are considered more outlandish than those of other people.

Origins: First recorded in the mid-20th century, the phrase was famously used by The New Yorker to describe wartime Prime Minister Sir Winston Churchill.

Example: With her outlandish fashion, she was someone larger than life.

Lead someone by the nose

Meaning: Control someone totally, especially by deceiving them.

Origin: This expression was inspired by the idea of an animal that is controlled by its sense of smell. It was also used as an expression by Shakespeare in Othello where he wrote "'The Moor...will as tenderly be led by th'nose As asses are".

Example: The tempest led them by the nose and now they are stuck on her island forever.

Lead someone up the garden path

Meaning: Give someone misleading clues or signals.

Origin: This expression was used in the early 20th century. It was believed that during these times, someone would often seduce their person out into the garden.

Example: He led me up the garden path. I thought he would offer me a great deal.

Leaps and bounds

Meaning: Grow or increase rapidly; Get better or improve in a short time

Origin: This idiom originated during the time of Shakespeare. However, the expression was first used to express disbelief or surprise. But as the years passed, its meaning changed to mean "improving in the shortest amount of time."

Example: She had grown leaps and bounds in height.

Leave no stone unturned

Meaning: To make every effort possible to accomplish an aim

Origin: When the Persians were defeated by the Greeks at Plataea, Polycrates heard the rumor of a treasure being left by the Persian General Mardonius. Unable to find the treasures, Polycrates went to the Oracle at Delphi and asked for her help. He was told to move every stone in the area.

Example: Leave no stone unturned, we need to find mom's engagement ring before she comes home.

Leave someone to their own devices

Meaning: Someone to do as they wish without supervision.

Origin: The word "device" was used to describe the word inclination or fancy. This expression was first cited in the book called General Confession in the Book of Common Prayer.

Example: I'm going to leave you guys to your devices for now.

Let one's hair down

Meaning: To relax or behave in an uninhibited manner.

Origin: This expression was taken from some of the practices of women in 1655. Women are required to pull their hair up, especially on certain occasions. However, they would often let their hair down when it's nighttime or when they are at home.

Example: You don't have to hide; let your hair down.

Let someone have it

Meaning: Attack someone physically or verbally

Origin: This expression was the crucial outcome of one of the notorious English murder trials. In late 1952, Derek Bentley and Christopher Craig attempted to rob a warehouse but were trapped by the police. Craig pulled a gun out while Bentley, who was apprehended, shouted "Let him have it, Chris!" This misleading phrase killed Bentley and imprisoned Craig because he was underage.

Example: Let someone have it, especially if they asked for it.

Let the cat out of the bag

Meaning: Divulge a secret.

Origin: This idiom first came to be in the 16th century. During that time many farmers would deceive people by selling a cat instead of a piglet. If a buyer opened the bag, he would uncover the farmer's deceit.

Example: She let the cat out of the bag and the party was no longer a surprise.

Let the dead bury the dead

Meaning: Not to grieve about the past and live in the present.

Origin: This expression was inspired by the Bible. It was taken from a gospel where a disciple had asked Jesus' permission to let him leave and bury his father. However, Jesus responded, "Follow Me, Let the dead bury their own dead." (Matthew 8:22, NIV.)

Example: Let the dead bury the dead. We all need to move forward with our current predicament.

Lick into shape

Meaning: To give form to something, to make something or someone presentable

Origin: In ancient times, people believed that bears often give birth to a formless lump of flesh. Mother bears had to lick these cubs into a tiny version of a bear.

Example: The pot will be licked into shape until we succeed in making the perfect pot.

Lick one's wounds

Meaning: To recover from one's hurt feelings or defeat or harsh criticism.

Origin: This expression was taken from certain Greek and Roman beliefs. This belief stated that saliva has healing powers. This idea was also inspired by animals that usually lick their wounds to make them heal.

Example: She licked her wounds as she let another leader take the project.

Light at the end of the tunnel

Meaning: An indication that your suffering is nearing an end.

Origin: This expression was likened to the idea of a tunnel. Inside the tunnel, everything is dark but as soon as you are near the end, you will see a light seeping through.

Example: I can finally see the light at the end of the tunnel! All my hard work has finally paid off.

Light years

Meaning: A long distance.

Origin: The word light-years often refers to the distance the light can travel in a year.

Example: The distance between us is like lightyears away.

Lightbulb moment

Meaning: A moment of inspiration.

Origin: Inspired by the allusion to a light bulb turning on.

Example: I think I just had a lightbulb moment.

Lighten up

Meaning: Take it easy and relax

Origin: This expression was taken from ancient English belief. It talks about a person's heart being weighed after they die. A person with a light heart is believed to go to heaven while the otherwise will go straight down to hell.

Example: Lighten up, maybe your test wasn't really that bad, you know.

Lightning never strikes twice

Meaning: The same calamity never occurs twice.

Origin: This expression refers to the popular belief that lightning never strikes the same spot twice.

Example: They say the lightning never strikes twice, but look at us now.

Like a bolt from the blue

Meaning: Totally unexpectedly

Origin: This expression referred to the bolt of lightning that happened on a clear day. There was no explanation of the said event. However, people continuously use this expression to refer to something unexpected.

Example: Everything happened like a bolt from the blue.

Like a lamb to the slaughter

Meaning: As a helpless victim

Origin: This Biblical idiom was written in the Book of Daniel 53:7: 'he is brought as a lamb to the slaughter.'

Example: Gina was led like a lamb to the slaughter.

Like a leech

Meaning: Persistently or clingingly present.

Origin: This expression is likened to a leech who has attached itself to a person or animal. This parasite draws blood from its host and is difficult to remove once they are attached to the skin and feeding.

Example: This woman is like a leech clinging to my arm.

Like death warmed over

Meaning: Extremely tired or ill

Origin: This expression was originally a military slang that was used in the 1930s.

Example: Her expression looks very pale, like death warmed over.

Live on your hump

Meaning: Be self-sufficient. informal

Origin: The image here is of the camel, which is famous for surviving on the fat in its hump without feeding or drinking.

Example: Kids, when you grow up live on your hump.

Live or lead a dog's life

Meaning: A miserable and unpleasant life; to lead a drab or boring life

Origin: This expression was first cited in the 16th century in a manuscript. This manuscript showed an allusion to the miserable subservient existence of dogs during this era. The proverb "It's a dog's life, hunger, and ease." was coined from this expression.

Example: My parents used to tell me that they used to live a dog's life.

Living hand to mouth

Meaning: Not knowing when the next meal would come from

Origin: This expression was first coined during the Great Famine in Great Britain during the 16th century. During this time, people would grab the food by hand and place it immediately into their mouths.

Example: Beggars are living hand to mouth in the streets.

Living on borrowed time

Meaning: Limited lifespan

Origin: This expression was taken from the idea of borrowed time in 17th century England. "Borrowers time" often refers to the first eleven days of May which happens to be part of April in the old style calendar. It was only in the 1880s when the expression referred to death in both the US and Great Britain.

Example: All the living things on Earth are living" on borrowed time.

Lock horns

Meaning: Engage in conflict.

Origin: This expression was taken from the image of two bulls fighting head-to-head with their horns.

Example: It is normal for people to lock horns from time to time.

Lock, stock, and barrel

Meaning: The whole thing

Origin: This expression is similar to "line, hook, and sinker". However, this expression was derived from the three parts of the musket. A musket is a gun that uses a lock or a latch to release firing.

Example: We got everything lock, stock, and barrel.

Lone it

Meaning: To do an activity alone

Origin: This expression was first cited in the early 1960s. It was written in S.E Hinton's book called "The Outsider". Since then, it has become a popular phrase.

Example: They wanted to hang out with him today, but he decided to lone it and stay at the dorms this weekend.

Long run

Meaning: In the distant future

Origin: This idiom dates back to the early 1600s. It was taken from the idea that a runner will continue running until he reaches the finish line. Since then, it has been used figuratively.

Example: You will be able to experience the fruit of your hard work in the long run.

Long shot

Meaning: An attempt that has little chance of success

Origin: This idiom was first used in naval warfare during the 1800s. Long shot referred to the cannons used as major weapons. However, as effective as they can be, their aims are often inaccurate. Apart from that, cannonballs can only travel short distances. Because of this many battles would often take place in close quarters. However, if there are cannonballs that are fired outside the normal range it is considered a long shot and most are likely to fail.

Example: He decided to take the long shot even if he wasn't sure how it would end.

Long time no see, it's a long time

Meaning: Since we last met (used as a greeting).

Origin: This idiom developed as a humorous imitation of broken English spoken by a Native American.

Example: Long time no see, it's a long time since we last saw each other.

Look daggers at

Meaning: Glare angrily or venomously at.

Origin: This expression was taken from Shakespeare's Hamlet. He used this expression when he reproached his mother.

Example: Leo looks daggers at his mother, who was feet away.

Look on the bright side

Meaning: To be positive and optimistic despite problems

Origin: This expression dates back to 1932 in a British Musical Comedy titled "Looking on the Bright Side." This play tells the story of two lovers who are into music acts. But when one of them got a taste of fame, he left his lover for another actress.

Example: Look on the bright side, you may not get the high mark that you were aiming for but you didn't fail the test.

Look what the cat dragged in

Meaning: To call attention to someone who has just entered the area.

Origin: The expression may not have a clear origin on how it started but it was said that it was inspired by cats who loved gifting them with their prey.

Example: Look what the cat dragged in today? Hi Jamie! That was a grand entrance, if I may say.

Loose cannon

Meaning: An unpredictable person or out of control.

Origin: In the 1600s, cannons were mounted on the decks of ships. Cannons were the primary weapons used in naval warships. They are often secured by ropes to avoid cannons from moving during voyages. However, during rough weather or when there was a violent recoil, cannons would sometimes break free from their restraints. The loose cannons caused major damage to the ship and injuries to the sailors.

Example: They said he was a loose cannon because of his idealistic belief.

Loose lips sink ships

Meaning: Be careful what you say, for it may fall upon the wrong ears and be used against you

Origin: This expression was first cited in WWII in an American Slogan. The slogan encouraged people to be cautious about what information they tell. The information may fall into the wrong hands.

Example: This information is confidential. Loose lips sink ships.

Lose face

Meaning: Suffer a loss of respect; be humiliated.

Origin: This expression was a direct translation from the Chinese idiom 'tiu lien"

Example: The team of swimmers lost face after losing the title of the champions.

Lose your marbles

Meaning: Go insane; become irrational or senile

Origin: In this context, the word "marble" refers to one's mental faculties. This expression was used as an American slang which has an underlying reference to a children's game called marbles.

Example: They had lost their marbles after being discredited for their works.

Lost in thought

Meaning: Thinking of something; mentally absent because of a certain thought.

Origin: This expression is often used on people who are always looking blankly into something. They call this look "lost in thought."

Example: She was lost in thought for a bit before she perked up and told us another story.

Lower (or drop or let down) your guard

Meaning: Relax your defensive posture, leaving yourself vulnerable to attack.

Origin: This expression was taken from boxing. Boxers would often put their guards up because their opponents were often unpredictable.

Example: It's okay. You can lower your guard down. It's just me.

Lower the bar

Meaning: To lower standards or expectations

Origin: Lower the bar is an expression that originates from the athletic event called the High Jump. In this sport, the lower the bar, the easier it is to jump over. The higher the bar, the more challenging it is to jump over.

Example: We should lower the bar on the designs, you know.

M)

Mad as a hatter

Meaning: To be crazy

Origin: This idiom comes with two references. One of them refers to the Mad Hatter in the story Alice in Wonderland. However, this idiom was first used during the 17th and 18th centuries. During this time in France, many hat makers would use mercury when making hats. The mercury caused massive poisoning that drove many people mad.

Example: He became mad as a hatter after his family died from the accident.

Make a deadset at

Meaning: Make a determined attempt to win the affection of.

Origin: This expression dated from the early 19th century. Originally, this expression was used to describe a dog's behavior during a sporting game where they point their muzzle or tail in a certain direction of the game.

Example: She is dead set on winning this contest.

Make a hash of

Meaning: Make a mess of; bungle.

Origin: The word hash is taken from the French verb "hacher" which means 'chop up small'. A hash is a dish with cooked meat cut into small tiny pieces. It is then re-cooked with gravy to add more flavor. Figuratively, this expression is also used to denote "mess" in a derogatory way.

Example: I accidentally made a hash out of the software.

Make all the difference

Meaning: Influence someone or something in a positive way

Origin: This expression dates back to the 1500s. It came from the Bible in the Book of Leviticus 11:47. In this chapter, it talks about how to depict the clean and holy from the dirty and unclean.

Example: Small acts of kindness can make all the difference.

Make one's mouth water

Meaning: Something that one could wish that they could have

Origin: It was first recorded in 1555 from a reference by Richard Eden who was writing about cannibals in the book New Worlde. He wrote, "These crafty foxes beganne to swallow theyr spettle as thyre mouthes watered for greediness of theyr prey."

Example: This fun game will definitely make your mouth water from the excitement.

Make or break

Meaning: The factor which decides whether something will succeed or fail.

Origin: This expression comes from the British English "is make or mar" which was recorded in the 15th century. However, it was only in the mid-19th century when the word "make or break" became a popular variant of the phrase.

Example: Make or break, I am glad we went this far.

Make someone's blood boil

Meaning: To make someone extremely angry

Origin: It was first cited in Alcibiades by Thomas Otway that was published in England in 1675. He wrote, "I am impatient and my blood boils high."

Example: Her airheadedness can make someone's blood boil.

Make someone's day

Meaning: make an otherwise ordinary or dull day pleasingly memorable for someone.

Origin: This expression was first cited in the movie Sudden Impact where the character Dirty Harry said Go ahead, make my day.

Example: He loves to make her day.

Make someone's hackles rise

Meaning: Make someone angry or indignant.

Origin: Hackles often refers to the feather on the neck of a fighting cock. It also refers to the hair on top of the dog's head. These hackles would often raise when an animal is excited or angry

Example: They like to make my hackle rise.

Making up leeway

Meaning: Falling behind or wasting time

Origin: This expression is taken from a ship drifting off course.

Example: We should stop making up leeways or we won't be able to finish this order on time.

Making waves

Meaning: Creating troubles or problems

Origin: This expression was taken from the 1900s when waves are one of the things that power a boat. However, waves created by other heavily laden boats can cause problems with smaller and lighter boats.

Examples: The tourists are making waves at the beach.

Marching orders

Meaning: A dismissal or sending off.

Origin: This military idiom refers to the instructions of the superior officers before the troops depart for a mission or for war.

Example: He gave us our marching orders before we were sent to war.

Mark someone's card

Meaning: Give someone information.

Origin: This idiom dates back to the mid-20th century. It was taken from horse racing. The card in this context refers to the race card with a list of horses in a certain race. If you happen to mark the card, you are giving tips to the possible winners of the race.

Example: I can mark your card for some secret information that you might need in the future.

Meet a deadline

Meaning: To finish something in time.

Origin: This idiom originated during the American Civil War. The deadline referred to the line drawn 20 feet from the inside wall of the stockade where the prisoners were kept. If the prisoners crossed the deadline, accidentally or not, they would be shot to death.

Example: Sara has to meet the deadline of her homework if she wants to pass.

Meet your maker

Meaning: Die.

Origin: This expression was an allusion to the Christian belief that once a person dies, his soul will be judged by God.

Example: Maybe it's time that you meet your maker.

Middle of the road

Meaning: A position midway between two extremes, a safe position

Origin: This expression originated during the days when pavements were not yet invented. During this time, the safer way to walk along the street was by walking in the middle of the road.

Example: She was in the middle of the road before the argument started.

Mind your own beeswax

Meaning: Mind your own business

Origin: During the olden days, many women would use bee's wax to help them solve acne problems. They would use a thin layer of beeswax as their skin care routine. The usage of this idiom started when many women started to stare at their reflections more often..

Example: You need to learn to mind your own beeswax instead of listening to these nonsense.

Miss the boat

Meaning: Missed out an opportunity because of ignorance

Origin: This idiom comes from a biblical story in Genesis 6:9—8:22, Noah's Ark, This reference referred to the people who didn't heed Noah's warning about the Great Flood. These people have washed away.

Example: Don't miss the boat on this promotion. You might not be given another chance again.

Money for old rope

Meaning: A quick and easy way to earn money.

Origin: This expression is dated to the 17th and 18th centuries. Once the ship returned to shore, sailors would assess the riggings of the ships to know whether or not they were still in good condition to travel. If the riggings were damaged during the voyage, they were removed. If some sails were good but not seaworthy, they were sold onshore. The captain of the ship would sometimes give the authority to senior crew members to sell old ropes. The senior crew was able to make money out of old rope.

Example: Selling your old clothes is like money for old rope.

Monkey see monkey do

Meaning: Mimicking someone's action

Origin: This expression dated back to February 1922 in The Transactions of the Commonwealth Club of California. They were celebrating the psychological law that was discovered by the philosopher and mathematician Pythagoras of Samos.

Example: One way to teach your child is by monkey see, monkey do.

More haste, less speed

Meaning: You make better progress with a task if you don't try to do it too quickly.

Origin: Initially, this expression is used to denote speed. It was taken from the proverb 'success in the performance of an activity.'

Example: More haste, and less speed will give you a better routine on your projects.

More or less

Meaning: Approximate

Origin: This expression is one of the oldest idioms in the English Language. It was first cited in 1225 in one of the notable anonymous prose works of Ancren Riwle which he wrote "More oder lesse."

Example: There are 55,000, more or less, people in the venue.

More than your job's worth

Meaning: Not worth risking your job for.

Origin: This phrase was first used as "jobsworth." This word is applied to a minor official who says 'it's more than my job's worth.' They often used this phrase to justify the insistence of petty rules even at the expense of common sense.

Example: Are you sure that this is more than your job's worth?

Move into high gear

Meaning: Immediate increase inactivity

Origin: It was derived from a straight transmission which was invented for early automobiles. Earlier automobiles needed to be changed manually to perform better. Hence, the expression was coined.

Example: We need to move into high gear if we want to hit the quota.

Move mountains

Meaning: Achieve spectacular and apparently impossible results: Make every possible effort

Origin: This expression was taken from 1 Corinthians 13:2 where it was written as 'And though I have the gift of prophecy, and understand all mysteries, and all knowledge; and though I have all faith so that I could remove mountains, and have no charity, I am nothing'.

Example: They want to move mountains with their goals.

Mumbo jumbo

Meaning: Nonsense, something that has no meaning

Origin: This expression was taken from Francis Moore's book called Travel into the Inland Part of Africa. He first cited the expression as "A dreadful Bugbear to the Women, call'd Mumbo-Jumbo, which is what keeps the Woman In awe."

Example: Please stop with this mumbo jumbo.

My name is mud

Meaning: Extremely unpopular person.

Origin: This idiom was taken from the history of Abraham Lincoln's assassination by John Wilkes Booth. When Booth tried to escape after committing murder, he was injured. He was treated by Dr. Samuel Mudd, who was also President Lincoln's physician. Since then, he was considered a co-conspirator of Lincoln's assassination. However, the case was dismissed because of the lack of evidence. Up to this date, there are still debates on whether or not Dr. Mudd is considered innocent or a murderer. Hence the expression was created.

Example: My name is mud. People don't really like me.

Nail a lie

Meaning: Expose something as a falsehood or deception.

Origin: This expression refers to shopkeepers nailing forged coins to their shop counter to expose them and put them out of circulation, or to farmers.

Example: Journalists have nailed a lie as they discovered some of the hidden stories of our history.

Nail in the coffin

Meaning: An action or event that will help bring about the death, end, or failure of something or someone

Origin: This idiom was an allusion of a corpse being nailed into the wooden coffin and is trapped until someone removes the nails. This expression has been used since the mid-1700s where it was also cited in The Taunton Courier in September 1812.

Example: The medical results were the nail in the coffin; John won't be able to dance professionally anymore.

Nail your colors to the mast

Meaning: To display one's beliefs defiantly.

Origin: This expression is coined from naval warfare. In the 18th century, one way to tell the ship's position was through its color. If the color of the ship was raised on the mainmast, it meant that the battleship was ready to fight. But if it was lowered down, it meant that the ship was surrendering. Because of the fear of death, many sailors would lower their color to save themselves. Captains would often nail their colors to stop sailors from surrendering their ships to enemies.

Example: We will nail our colors to the mast! We will never give up on our goal!

Near the knuckle

Meaning: On the indecent or offensive.

Origin: This expression was coined in the late 19th century when it was referred to as close to the permitted limit of behavior.

Example: Their remarks and unwarranted comments are downright near the knuckle.

Never had it so good

Meaning: Have never before enjoyed such prosperity.

Origin: This idiom was probably coined by George Meany. However, it was only used popularly when Conservative Prime Minister of England Harold Macmillan added this expression in 1957.

Example: She never had it so good.

Night owl

Meaning: A night person; a person who is awake at night

Origin: This expression refers to a person who has the characteristics of an owl. Owls are nocturnal creatures that often hunt at night.

Example: Don't worry about getting home late. Liz is a night owl, she will open the door for you when you get home.

Nightmare dressed like a daydream

Meaning: Describes something that seems very pleasant or attractive at first but eventually reveals itself as horrible. It may also describe a person who is sweet at first glance but is evil

Origin: This expression was taken from Irish and Scottish folklore. This folklore talks about an attractive woman by day and a scary monster by night. This expression was then popularized in a song called "Blank Space" by Taylor Swift where she likened herself to a nightmare dressed like a daydream.

Example: John was a nightmare dressed like a daydream.

No holds barred

Meaning: Without restriction, with no regard to fairness, by any means possible

Origin: This expression was a wrestling term that refers to the no-holds-barred contest. In this contest, players are allowed to throw or lift their opponents following the rules and restrictions of wrestling.

Example: The witness told us the whole truth with no holds barred.

No pain, no gain

Meaning: It is necessary to work hard or strive to reap rewards; suffer to achieve results

Origin: This expression is also a known proverb in the 2nd Century. This expression was taken from the Ethics of the Fathers, the Rabbi writes: "According to the pain is the gain."

Example: No pain, no gain, always remember that.

No room to swing a cat

Meaning: Very cramped

Origin: This idiom used to be a practice in the 16th century wherein cats were placed inside a sack and used as a moving target for archers. The phrase came to be in Shakespeare's Much Ado About Nothing. In this, he stated that there was no room for such practice.

Another common theory of this idiom is that it talks about the cat-o-nine-tails and not the actual cat. The cat-o-nine-tails was a whip that was used by the British Navy to punish soldiers. The expression "no room to swing a cat" referred to the cramped condition of the ship and that it's difficult to go through with the punishment.

Example: There is no room to swing a cat on this bus. I can hardly move.

No spring chicken

Meaning: No longer young

Origin: This expression was taken from a certain practice of chicken farmers. In the past, chickens that were born in spring were priced higher compared to chickens that were born before the previous winter. This would suggest that the chicken that had gone through one winter is considered older.

Example: My nephew is no spring chicken anymore.

No walk in the park

Meaning: Not an easy task

Origin: Started during the mid-20th century. This expression was likened to a "walk in the park" This activity is considered a relaxing leisure activity.

Example: Parenting is no walk in the park.

None of your lip

Meaning: to ask someone to stop speaking

Origin: This expression originated in Medieval England. There were several arguments on where this word originated. However, given the mannerism of the 1800s, it is possible that the word "none of your lip" is synonymous with the phrase "shut-up".

Example: None of your lip! I don't ever want to talk about this topic again!

Not my cup of tea

Meaning: Something that you don't enjoy but can relate to.

Origin: This expression goes back to 1939. It was used figuratively in a book called The Amazing Theater by James Agate. He wrote "It was preceded by 'he's my cup of tea.'

Example: Partying is not my cup of tea.

Not on my watch

Meaning: It means that nothing will happen while this certain person is in charge.

Origin: This nautical expression was taken from the day and night watches on the ship. The lookout or the watcher is in charge of whatever happens during their shift.

Example: No one is going to fail the test, not on my watch.

Not the sharpest tool in the shed

Meaning: Slow person, not the smartest person.

Origin: This expression's origin remains unclear. However, in this expression, the word "sharpness" is associated with mental quickness. This expression was first coined in the 1990s.

Example: I may not be the sharpest tool in the shed, but I can empathize with what he feels he feels.

Not to mince matters/one's words

Meaning: To speak frankly, to be brutally honest

Origin: This expression was inspired by the act of mincing the meat to make it easier to eat. Figuratively, it means that someone who doesn't mince their words will give you a hard truth.

Example: Jada does not mince her words. She will tell you exactly what went wrong.

Not worth a flip

Meaning: Totally worthless

Origin: It originated during the late 19th century. It was derived from flipping one's finger. It was then used in a printed reference called Great Hours in a poem called Making it Skip. It was written as "Now somehow, that is our Charlie's way. He takes little troubles that vex one so, Not worth a flip, And makes them seem to frolic and play."

Example: This painting is fake. It is not worth a flip.

O)

Of a certain age

Meaning: Not specifying a certain or actual age.

Origin: This idiom was first recorded in 1754. It was said that it may have been inspired by the French "d'un certain age."

Example: When ladies are of a certain age, they are ready to get married.

Off the beaten track

Meaning: Not the usual path

Origin: This expression was often used in places that many people don't usually go. This expression is often used by travel agencies whenever they talk about destinations that are less popular but equally beautiful.

Example: There are tons to see in the off-the-beaten tracks that are seldom taken.

Off the hook

Meaning: No longer in trouble or difficulty; (of a telephone receiver) not on its rest, and so not receiving incoming calls.

Origin: This expression has been used figuratively since the 15th century. It used to be a nautical expression likened to a fish who has been caught by a fishing hook. Another origin of this expression was first used in the 19th century. It was likened to the telephone receiver that literally hung on a hook.

Example: I am glad that I am off the hook on this one.

Off the record

Meaning: Sharing the information within group of people and should not be repeated to other people

Origin: This expression was first coined by President Franklin Roosevelt in 1932. During those times, he wasn't really comfortable with the formal setting during the interviews. There were times that he would request to speak "off the record" to joke with the audience, and not focus on the serious topics for a few minutes.

Example: Don't worry, everything is off the record.

Off to a flying start

Meaning: A good beginning

Origin: This is inspired by yacht racing. A yacht has a flying start based on its position and impeccable timing as it crosses the start line at the closest starting time possible.

Example: We are off to a flying start with this journey.

Old school (and also old skool)

Meaning: Conservative beliefs; Outdated: Someone very traditional

Origin: This expression dates back to the 19th century. It was first cited in 1852 in a novel by Charles Dickens. It was only in the later years that this expression was coined into Old Skool where it refers to the hiphop music in the late 1980s

Example: I'm old school when it comes to marriage and relationships.

On a high

Meaning: In a state of euphoria.

Origin: This expression was originally from mid-20th-century US slang, referring specifically to the euphoria induced by drugs.

Example: Everyone was on a high after that energetic performance.

On cloud nine

Meaning: Supremely happy

Origin: There are several origins of this expression. However, the closest would be the ancient significance of the number three. If you square three, you would get the number 9.

Example: I feel like I'm walking on cloud nine.

On edge

Meaning: Nervous; irritable

Origin: This expression was taken from another expression which " to set one's teeth on edge" means to make the person nervous.

Example: We were all on edge while waiting for the news.

On hand

Meaning: Present, nearby, close, or easily accessible: ready to help

Origin: There is no clear history for this expression. Most etymologists believe that the expression is very much literal.

Example: We have all the ingredients on hand.

On pins and needles

Meaning: Tense and anxious; to be nervous

Origin: This expression was taken from the early 1800s. It refers to the uncomfortable sensation on your flesh when you are recovering from numbness.

Example: Everyone backstage is on pins and needles.

On tenterhooks

Meaning: In a state of suspense or agitation because of uncertainty about a future event.

Origin: In the past, the tenter had a different design that used hooks and nails fixed around the tenter. Figuratively, the expression came to be in the 18th century when it was used to mean "an agitated state of mind"

Example: Dahlia left me on tenterhooks when she left without saying anything about the new project. How am I going to finish it?

On the ball

Meaning: Alert to new trends, ideas, and methods; Knowledgeable and competent

Origin: This expression was taken from a specific ball game. Players were asked to keep their eyes on the ball. Since then, this expression has been used even in current times. Its oldest citation was in 1864.

Example: We were on the ball for an upcoming drama release. We are excited that we can advertise it.

On the fiddle

Meaning: Cheating on someone.

Origin: This expression comes with a nautical origin. Dining tables on ships often have raised edges called "fiddles". Fiddles are used to prevent plates from sliding off the table during rough seas. Sailors would eat on the wooden plates that were built with their own fiddles. If the sailor was overfilling their plates and that it was going over their own fiddle, meant that the sailor was on the fiddle.

Example: Sara was caught on the fiddle after they saw something wrong with the ledger.

On the horns of a dilemma

Meaning: Faced with a decision involving equally unfavorable alternatives.

Origin: This expression was taken from the Latin phrase "argumentum cornutum" which is translated as a "horned argument."The idea behind this expression is that you were able to avoid the horn of the problem but accidentally added another horn instead.

Example: I didn't expect to be on the horns of a dilemma.

On the mat

Meaning: Being reprimanded by someone in authority.

Origin: This expression is a military idiom that talks about the orderly room mat that an accused soldier would stand on in front of his commanding officer.

Example: We were all pulled on the mat for not following our marching orders.

On the right track

Meaning: To do something correctly or well.

Origin: This expression didn't talk about the track but "tack." A ship is the "on the right tack" if it follows a zig-zag path, angling from left to right as it moves forward. This course is known as tacking". This technical art can help the ship move on the right tack with the right amount of wind on its sails.

Example: You are on the right track towards your goal.

On the rocks

Meaning: Having problems in the relationship.

Origin: This expression was taken from a naval context. It talks about ships being grounded on the rocks and breaking apart. It was only in the late 1800s that this expression was used to refer to the rocks and breaking apart relationships.

Example: Our relationship has been on the rocks for a couple of days.

On the same page

Meaning: The people involved share the same understanding or agreement of the same idea.

Origin: The phrase first began during the middle of the mid-20th century. It was taken from the idea that everyone was looking at the same page of the document that they were given.

Example: We all have to be on the same page during the presentation.

On the tapis

Meaning: (Of a subject) under consideration or discussion.

Origin: This expression is a partial translation of the French phrase "sur le tapis", meaning literally 'on the carpet'. A carpet in this context is a covering for a table rather than a floor, as indeed it was originally in the English idiom "on the carpet." It refers to the covering of the council table around which a matter would be debated.

Example: I can't decide on this matter for now. Should I put it on the tapis for the time being?

On the tip of my tongue

Meaning: Something that you intended to say but forgot before you could say it.

Origin: It was originally from the French expression "presque vu" which means 'almost seen'. This expression was first referred to as a psychological phenomenon by William James who was able to experience it.

Example: I wanted to tell you something but I think it's stuck on the tip of my tongue.

On the warpath

Meaning: Ready and eager for confrontation.

Origin: The phrase originated with reference to Native Americans heading towards a battle with an enemy.

Example: Mira was on the warpath when she saw the thief who stole her parts.

On top of the world

Meaning: Feeling happy and delighted; in a good mood as everything is going well for you

Origin: Dates back to the 20th century. Many writers have been using this expression. However, there was no clear origin on how this expression came to be.

Example: My father was on top of the world when he knew my mother was pregnant with me.

On your uppers

Meaning: Extremely short of money.

Origin: This expression was inspired by worn-out shoes. In the past, people could tell the class of the person through their shoes. If your shoes are worn out, it means to say you are having problems with money.

Example: After spending all my money on online shopping, I'm currently on my uppers.

One of these days

Meaning: At some unspecified time in the future.

Origin: It was cited in the P.G. Wodehouse Ukridge in 1924 where it was written as 'Don't you worry, you'll get your money back ... ' 'When?' 'One of these days,' said Ukridge, buoyantly. 'One of these days.'

Example: One of these days, I will finally be able to clear my closet.

One over the eight

Meaning: Slightly drunk.

Origin: Taken from the idea that a person can be drunk after drinking 8 glasses of beer. This expression is known to be military slang in the early 20th century.

Example: They were all one over the eight. I can't imagine how I would drive them all tonight.

One smart cookie

Meaning: Someone with great tenacity

Origin: Although the origin of this expression is still unknown, some people would believe that this expression was often used by men to refer to an attractive and smart woman.

Example: Your daughter is one smart cookie.

Other fish to fry

Meaning: To not be interested in something because you have more important, interesting, or profitable things to do

Origin: This expression was inspired by the Spanish novel Don Quixote. This expression was first cited by Sancho "this is no time for me to mind niceties, and spelling of letters: I have other fish to fry."

Example: There are other fish to fry. I don't think I should be doing this now.

Out like a light

Meaning: Sleeping heavily or unconscious

Origin: This expression was taken from the idea of turning off the lights.

Example: The baby is out like a light after crying his heart out all day long.

Out of kilter

Meaning: Out of harmony or balance.

Origin: The word kilter dates back to the 17th century. It was defined as 'frame or order'. It was only in the later years that it was used as an expression.

Example: The cat suddenly jumping in the dance threw us out of kilter.

Out of the blue

Meaning: It happened suddenly

Origin: This expression was first coined during the French Revolution in 1837. It was written as "Arrestment, suddenly really as a bolt out of the Blue, has hit strange victims." The said expression was also similar to the expression 'like a lightning bolt.'

Example: Out of the blue, a stampede happened.

Out of the gate

Meaning: From the very beginning

Origin: It referred to the horses coming out of the gate during the race. Its first printed reference was dated back to 1981 by Lawrence Lee in the book called "The Grant's Game". He wrote,"If you said yes to all four of these questions, you look like a winner right out of the gate."

Example: She was the first one out of the gate.

Out of the woods

Meaning: Out of danger

Origin: There are several origins when it comes to this idiom. However, its origin came from a proverb that was referenced in the papers of Benjamin Franklin.

Example: It seems the patient is out of the woods.

Outside the lines

Meaning: Not sticking to the rules; live or follow a non-traditional lifestyle.

Origin: The idea of this expression often refers to children's coloring books. These books are often pre-printed with pictures. Children are tasked by their educators to color inside the lines and not outside the lines. Since then it has been used figuratively.

Example: People often wonder why she decided to live outside the lines.

Over the moon

Meaning: Extremely happy; delighted

Origin: Inspired by an old nursery rhyme where it was written in the lines "Heigh diddle diddle, the cat and the fiddle, the cow jumped over the moon."

Example: She was over the moon to learn that she passed the licensure test.

Over the top

Meaning: Excessive, too much

Origin: This expression originated during trench warfare in WWI. To launch an attack, many of the soldiers would have to climb out of their trench to fire at their enemies. Trenches were sandbags piled up together to create a barrier for soldiers during the shootouts.

Example: You went over the top, we are only going to walk the dogs.

Pandora's box

Meaning: Forbidden secrets or information that can cause harm.

Origin: This was inspired by Greek Mythology. Pandora was the first woman created by Zeus and the wife of Epimetheus. They were given a mysterious box and were told that no one should open it. Pandora opened the box and released all the evils into the world.

Example: They feared that Pandora's Box would open and cause more chaos in their current situation.

Pass the torch

Meaning: To pass on the responsibility or task to another person

Origin: This expression was taken from the early 1800s. Originally, it was taken from a Greek race where runners would pass the torch from one person to another.

Example: Now that we are graduating, it is time to pass the torch of the student body to the new elected officers.

Pass with flying colors

Meaning: Success at a difficult task.

Origin: This expression dated back to the 1700s. During this era of exploration, the ship's flag was considered the "color". Whenever a naval ship or fleet was victorious in battle, the captain would raise its flag high above the mast as they sailed homeward bound. This would signify that the ship or fleet has successfully defeated the enemy.

Example: Daisy did well on her test. She passes with flying colors.

Pat on the back

Meaning: To praise or express appreciation for a job well done; compliment a person for his hard work.

Origin: This expression dates back during the 1800s where it used to refer to a literal pat on the back. However, in the current era, the idea of "pat on the back" is now accompanied with the idea of a reward.

Example: Give yourself a pat on the back for a job well done.

Pay lip service

Meaning: To agree by word of mouth only

Origin: This idiomatic expression was used to express the idea of agreeing or swearing loyalty for something not supporting it in action. This expression was first cited in the Book of Isaiah 29:3 where it was written as 'honoring God and Jesus only with one's lips.'

Example: Sadly, many officials would pay lip service to their stand about pollution and the environment."

Phone ringing off the hook

Meaning: Incessant ringing

Origin: It was first cited in a printed article from Milk Plant Monthly Volume 6 in 1957. It was written "The phone begins ringing off the hook... 'Susie won't drink her milk... my husband is going on a diet... the Dodgers lost three games in a row.' Today's youth have a new saying, 'blowing up my phone.'

Example: My phone is ringing off the hook.

Pick of the litter

Meaning: The first choice or getting the most popular item

Origin: This expression was derived from puppy picking practices. It originated during the mid-19th century when people picked greyhound puppies for hunting games.

Example: This bag was my pick of the litter.

Pie in the sky

Meaning: The promise that never quite materializes

Origin: This expression was coined by a US immigrant laborer called Joe Hill who was a member of a radical labor organization. He coined this expression in his parody song that criticized the Salvation Army's way of treating the poor.

Example: All that he is saying is pie in the sky.

Piece of cake

Meaning: Very easy

Origin: It was written in the 1930s by Ogden Nash. He had likened life to a piece of cake in his poem "The Primrose Path." People have been using this expression since then.

Example: My homework is a piece of cake!

Pipe down

Meaning: Request or command to be quiet.

Origin: This expression originally came from a signal from the boatswain's pipe. This signal is called piping down the hammock which means everyone should prepare for bedtime.

Example: I would like to ask everyone to pipe it down. We are going to start with the lessons very soon.

Piping hot

Meaning: Boiling hot

Origin: This expression was first used during Medieval times. It referred to the steam coming out of a spouted tea kettle which was first used in Mesopotamia. In the later years, Shakespeare used the word piping to describe bagpiping.

Example: Please be careful, your coffee is piping hot.

Play devil's advocate

Meaning: Take a side in an argument that is the opposite of what you really want or think.

Origin: This expression was taken from a Latin translation "advocatus diaboli" which is translated as "devil's advocate." This expression was often given to people or groups of people who are against the Roman Catholic Church.

Example: She plays as the devil's advocate in this case.

Play gooseberry

Meaning: Chaperone

Origin: This expression is inspired by the idea of couples who don't like being chaperoned. The gooseberry-picker is said to be the chaperon in this situation.

Example: I don't feel like playing gooseberry for couples during dates.

Play it by ear

Meaning: Spontaneous planning. Deciding along the way

Origins: This idiom started when a musician would play an instrument without referring to a music sheet. Many people used this phrase during the 16th century and it's been used even up to now.

Example: I don't really have plans today. I am going to play it by ear and see how it goes.

Play to the gallery

Meaning: Act in an exaggerated or histrionic manner, especially in order to appeal to popular taste.

Origin: This expression was first coined in the 17th century. During this time, the galleries are the cheapest and highest seating in a theater. Oftentimes, people of lower status would often get these seats when watching plays.

Example: I hate it when she plays to the gallery. People would think we are threatening her bad.

Poor as a church mouse

Meaning: Someone poor or impoverished

Origin: This expression was very popular during the 17th century. It was a famous tale about a mouse who took refuge in a church but died because of the lack of food.

Example: We were poor as a church mouse but look at us now.

Pop the question

Meaning: Proposing for marriage

Origin: This expression was first coined in 1725. It was often used in asking important questions. However, since 1826, this expression has been popularly used to refer to the idea of proposing marriage.

Example: Waldo finally popped the question to his long-term relationship after being together for more than 10 years.

Posh people

Meaning: People with style and money

Origin: This expression was first used during the 17th to 18th century when the Oriental Steam Navigation Company ferried people from England to India. During this trip, people were offered port cabins which became in demand with the passengers. So many companies like the Oriental Steam Navigation offered tickets with marks P.O.S.H or Port Out Starboard Home which are often afforded by the wealthy people.

Example: These posh people can buy everything they want anytime.

Post haste

Meaning: Immediately, with urgency

Origin: The expression post haste was inspired by the 16th-century postal system wherein messages were relayed by messengers on horseback. They would often shout the words "post haste" to get the attention of other messengers and send the packet to its destinations.

Example: Please send me your reply post haste.

Pot (or crock) of gold

Meaning: A large but distant or illusory reward.

Origin: This expression was taken from the traditional story of finding a pot of gold at the end of the rainbow.

Example: There is always a pot of gold at the end of the rainbow.

Practice what you preach

Meaning: Do the things that you tell others to do

Origin: This expression comes from a gospel in Matthew 23:3 where it says "So you must obey them and do everything they tell you. But do not do what they do, for they do not practice what they preach." It talks about following the laws but not following the Pharisees.

Example: Practice what you preach, your children see you as their role model.

Prick up your ears

Meaning: Pay attention to someone or something.

Origin: This expression was originally taken from the idea of horses and dogs who prick their ears up when they hear sounds in the background. It was only in 1626 when it was used in literary form by Francis Bacon.

Example: You have to prick up your ears in our Economics class or else you are going to fall behind.

Pros and cons

Meaning: The advantages and disadvantages

Origin: This phrase is considered a legal idiom. It refers to the "pros and contras." Pro argument allows the defendant to be granted bail. Contra argument is against granting the defendant bail.

Example: We need to weigh the pros and cons of buying a new car before going to the dealership.

Pull a fast one

Meaning: Try to gain an unfair advantage by the rapid action of some sort.

Origin: Originally coined in the early 20th century as a US slang.

Example: Sierra tried to pull a fast one on you.

Pull one out of the hat

Meaning: Bring off an unexpected trick in an apparently desperate situation.

Origin: The image here is of a rabbit pulled out of a magician's hat.

Example: Thankfully, she was able to pull one out of the hat.

Pull out all the stops

Meaning: To make a great effort to achieve something.

Origin: This idiom refers to the stops or knobs inside a pipe organ. To play the right tone and volume of the pipe organ, you need to play all the tones simultaneously.

Example: She had to pull out all the stops just to learn how to play the guitar.

Pull strings

Meaning: Make use of one's influence and contacts to gain an advantage unofficially or unfairly.

Origin: There are several references to this idiom but the closest one is 1904. It was an English translation of a French shorthand The Extraordinary Confessions of Diana Please by Bernard Edward Joseph Capes. It was written as "I have pulled some strings, sitting in my boudoir, with results as far-reaching as St. Stephen's."

Example: In other words, she knows someone who can pull some strings.

Pull the plug

Meaning: To bring an end or to kill someone.

Origin: This medical expression talks about people who use machines to keep them alive. If you pull the plug or turn off these machines, these people will die.

Example: After a heart-to-heart conversation, we decided to pull the plug on this relationship.

Pull your socks up

Meaning: To be determined; to be able to achieve the set target.

Origin: This phrase was coined from the idea of wearing special running shoes and socks for a race. Athletes would often pull their socks as a sign that they are ready for the race.

Example: It is time that you pull up your socks and do better on your next test.

Pushing up the daisies

Meaning: The dead and buried.

Origin: This humorous expression was used in the early 20th century as a euphemism of many daisy-related expressions concerning the grave.

Example: Because of my faith in God, I was able to stop pushing up the daisies.

Put a sock in it

Meaning: Rude way of telling people to behave

Origin: This expression came to be when soldiers would put a sock in an injured soldier's mouth to quiet him down.

Example: Mary had to put a sock on the noisy people on her floor.

Put your foot in it

Meaning: Say something (by mistake) that upsets, humiliates, or embarrasses someone

Origin: This expression dates back in the early 1700s. Originally, this expression was taken from a certain situation from the book 'Polite Conversation,' by Jonathan Swift where he wrote "The bishop has put his foot in it."

Example: You would never put your foot in it unless you want something from this restaurant.

Quit horsing around

Meaning: Stop doing mischievous antics

Origin: This animal-based idiom was taken from the word horseplay which means mischievous antics. Horses would often play in the pasture and corral. They would run, buck, and nip each other and wag their tails. This was likened to children whenever they play.

Example: Quit horsing around! Help me with the chores.

R)

Rabbit hole (down the rabbit hole)

Meaning: Mentally go somewhere surreal or strange. ; A weird, bizarre, or senseless situation, from which it is difficult to disengage.

Origin: It was inspired from the book Alice's Adventures in Wonderland. This expression was taken from the part where Alice falls down a rabbit hole and ends up in Wonderland, a weird and surreal place.

Example: When I listen to his music, my mind is always going down the rabbit hole.

Rags to riches

Meaning: Someone rises from being poor to become

Origin: This expression's origin is currently unknown. However, some people believe that this expression talks about describing people's clothes that have changed throughout time. From wearing rags, they changed their clothes after getting a lot of money.

Example: His rags to riches story inspired me to do better in my work.

Rain on someone's parade

Meaning: To disrupt someone's happy mood or attitude

Origin: This expression was likened to parades. Parades are joyous activities and are spent outside. However, the rain ruins the mood and the props for the parade.

Example: We were so excited but Jake just rained on our parade. Our reservation was canceled.

Rain or shine

Meaning: No matter what happens or what it takes; To be sure of something.

Origin: This idiom was first cited in 1699 by John Goad in his written work titled

Astro-meteorologica, or Aphorisms And Large Significant Discourses on the Natures and Influences of Celestial Bodies. He wrote, "In the meanwhile [sp] we are told our Aspect brings a Settlement as to what happens, Rain, Or Shine, for many days; but they leave the poor Disciple to determine the number himself."

Example: Rain or shine, you will see me waiting for you at the bus stop.

Raining cats and dogs

Meaning: Raining very hard

Origin: Originated during the 1500s when a huge rain came to England. People then usually had thatched roofs and saw cats and dogs falling from the roof. Thatched roofs were the source of warmth for cats and dogs during this era.

Example: It's raining cats and dogs. I can see the water level in the river going up.

Raise the bar

Meaning: To raise standards or expectations

Origin: This expression is the opposite of "lower the bar". It is inspired from the athletic event of pole vault and high jump. The higher the bar, the more challenging it is. The player with the highest bar wins the event.

Example: Athena's grades raise the bar for her college. Now everyone is expected to be like Athena.

Raring to go

Meaning: Anxious to go

Origin: This expression originated in 1909 when it was likened to horses that reared up their front feet from the ground. This act of the horses meant that they are excited and ready to run off once they are off the stake.

Example: They were all ready and raring to go.

Rat race

Meaning: Following a competitive but tiring route or routine.

Origin: This idiom was taken from the idea of rats that are in cages. These rats are given mazes that are tiring and filled with struggles.

Example: Everyone is all stuck in this rat race called life.

Recipe for success

Meaning: An attainable plan to get everything done with a positive result

Origin: This expression was created by Sir Walter Scott in one of his Waverly Novels. In one of his books, he wrote "A taking title, or the announcement of a popular subject, is a recipe for success much in favor with booksellers, but which authors will not always find efficacious."

Example: One ingredient in the recipe for success is to always do your best.

Red letter day

Meaning: A day to celebrate

Origin: It was inspired by a certain practice in the 15th century. People would mark all the holidays in red while the ordinary days were in black.

Example: Christmas is a Red Letter day

Red tape

Meaning: A complex procedure that can cause a delay in the process. It also refers to unnecessary files.

Origin: This idiom was dated during the 16th century. It talks about the documents that were bound in red tape which is difficult for clerks to access.

Example: This file is full of red tape.

Rest assured

Meaning: Emphasizing that there is no need to worry

Origin: Dating from the 1500s, it was used as a formal expression to express certainty and trust in a particular situation.

Example: Rest assured, we have everything under control.

Ride a tiger

Meaning: Take on responsibility or embark on a course of action that subsequently cannot safely be abandoned.

Origin: Originally taken from the Chinese proverb 'He who rides a tiger is afraid to dismount.'

Example: Soldiers often ride the tiger whenever there is war.

Ride out the storm

Meaning: Manage to survive a dangerous situation.

Origin: Riding out a storm is an expression where the captain of the vessel chooses to pursue a current course with a dangerous risk.

Example: We are ready to ride out the storm as long as we are together.

Riding shotgun

Meaning: To ride in the front seat of a vehicle.

Origin: Riding Shotgun originates in the Wild West. When driving a coach or a wagon, the driver is accompanied by another person carrying a shotgun. This way, they can protect themselves from bandits.

Example: I am riding shotgun in my mom's car.

Right around the corner

Meaning: Very near

Origin: This expression was taken on the literal idea of going around the other street. It was in 1921 that it was first used figuratively.

Example: I can feel summer is right around the corner.

Right off the bat

Meaning: Something happened immediately after it was started

Origin: This expression originated from baseball. However, it was only used as an actual idiom by George Putnam Upton in his Letters of Peregrine Pickle in 1869. He wrote, "The Devil is not only a hard hitter with the bat, but he is a quick fielder, and he will pick a soul right off the bat of one of these soft muscle men while S. M. is wasting his strength on the air."

Example: She was eliminated right off the bat.

Right up one's alley

Meaning: Someone's specialty

Origin: This idiom was first used by Francis Bacon during the 17th Century. He used this expression in his essay "Such men...are good but in their own Alley."

Example: Being cute is right up her alley.

Rip off

Meaning: The act of stealing; financial exploitation: Imitation or a fake product.

Origin: This expression was first coined by African Americans in 1904 as prison slang. But in the 1960s, people from the Haight Ashbury area in San Francisco started using this expression as part of their vernacular.

Example: This action figure is a rip-off! It doesn't look like Batman at all.

Rocket science

Meaning: Something overly complex

Origin: The word "rocket science" was an area of study that has been around since the Second World War. It talks about the allied troops capturing many German scientists and taking them to the US to help them with the American Rocket Science Program.

Example: Learning to drive is rocket science for me.

Rolling in dough

Meaning: Wealthy

Origin: The word "dough" is modern slang for money. However, this expression refers to a baking practice where doughs are rolled into layers of butter as part of the steps of making this pastry.

Example: Many social media influencers are not rolling in dough.

Rome wasn't built in a day

Meaning: Nothing good happens overnight

Origin: It was first coined in the 16th century by the British playwright and writer John Heywood. He used this expression in a certain dialogue in his work.

Example: Start your business small; after all Rome wasn't built in a day.

Room at the top

Meaning: Opportunity to join an elite or the top ranks of a profession.

Origin: This idiom was first attributed to the American politician, Daniel Webster (1782–1852). He was warned against attempting to enter the overcrowded legal profession. But Webster replied: 'There is always room at the top'.

Example: There is always a room at the top for you.

Rough it

Meaning: You have to live without the possessions and comforts that you normally have.

Origin: it was first recorded by Francis Grose in the book A Classical Dictionary of the Vulgar Tongue in 1785. It was written as "Rough, to lie rough, to lie all night in one's clothes; also roughing it."

Example: We can rough it out and keep trimming the articles until the whole template is complete.

Rub of the green

Meaning: The influence of luck.

Origin: The expression "rub of the green" originated in golf. This expression referred to an accidental interference with the position of the ball on the green or with the course. This expression was then used in the 1962 Guardian, stating "If applications. . . rub of the green."' reached fantastic proportions, the Government would have to consider the matter. 'At present, we treat it as a rub of the green.'

Example: He rubbed the green on everyone in the room. Everyone thinks they are lucky because of it.

Rub someone the wrong way

Meaning: To annoy or bother another person.

Origin: During colonial times, some Americans were very particular when it came to cleaning. Oftentimes, they would follow a specific way of cleaning the floorboards.

Rubbing the oak slabs the wrong way would result in the formation of streaks. The streaks would cause the floorboards to be ruined. This resulted in annoyed homeowners.

Example: Ces is mad at me for rubbing her the wrong way.

Rubber cheque

Meaning: A cheque that is returned unpaid.

Origin: This expression comes from the idea of bouncing cheques. Most cheques bounce because of insufficient funds in the drawer's account to cover them.

Example: Mrs.Woodburrow paid with a rubber cheque and it seems the shops are no longer happy about it.

Ruffle someone's feathers

Meaning: It means to irritate or annoy another person

Origin: It was originally taken from the fowls getting offensive when people rubbed their feathers.

Example: Siblings love to ruffle each other's feathers. This is how they show love for each other.

Rule of thumb

Meaning: Guesswork, rough calculation, an estimate based on experience rather than careful calculation

Origin: The phrase has been in figurative use since the late seventeenth century. From the tip of the thumb down to its joint measures is equal to inches. If you are able to get twelve thumbs, you will be able to get the exact measurement of one foot.

Example: It's a rule of thumb that you eat fewer calories to make it easier to lose weight.

Rule the roost

Meaning: be in complete control.

Origin: The expression was supposed to "rule the roast" which was common from the mid-16th century and onwards. This expression referred to someone being an important person at a banquet.

Example: I rule the roost in my expenses.

Run a tight ship

Meaning: To have someone or something under strict control

Origin: This expression refers to a strict captain running a disciplined crew. It also refers to a ship that is in tip-top condition and is ready for the voyage.

Example: We are running a tight ship on this project.

Run across

Meaning: Meet someone by accident; cross something while running

Origin: This expression was first cited in the book She Stoops to Conquer by Oliver Goldsmith. He wrote, "... you are to go sideways till you come upon Crack-Skull Common."

Example: She ran across several people today.

Run amok/amuck

Meaning: Behave in an unruly manner.

Origin: The word amok or amuck comes from the Malaysian word "amoq". Tribesmen used this word to describe someone who is attacking people who cross their path. People who exhibit this behavior are under the influence of opium. In the 17th century, people in England used the word amok or amuck colloquially to impress people.

Example: She was running amok because of the news.

Run high

Meaning: Be strong or tumultuous.

Origin: The image here is of waves or tides rising above their normal height, especially in stormy conditions.

Example: The waves unexpectedly ran high after several minutes.

Run interference

Meaning: Intervene on someone's behalf, typically so as to protect them from distraction or annoyance. North American informal

Original: This phrase was taken from American Football. Run interference was defined as blocking the opponent to clear a space for the ball carrier.

Example: Can you run interference and keep them distracted while we fix this?

Run into a brick wall

Meaning: Encountering insurmountable obstacles in achieving the desired goal

Origin: This idiom was first used in 1922 in the book called On Nature's Trail: A Wonder book In The Wild by F. St. Mars. It was likened to a bird that stopped dead as if she ran into a brick wall.

Example: We ran into a brick wall when we saw the amount of work in our midst.

S)

Saved by the bell

Meaning: Last-minute intervention, lucky escape

Origin: In boxing, bells are used to start and end around. This expression came to be when a boxer was able to escape a knockout due to the bell ending the current round.

Example: I was saved by the bell!

Sea change

Meaning: A change in perspective; undergo a complete transformation.

Origin: This expression was taken from the idea of how the weather changes. It was once mentioned in Shakespeare's The Tempest in 1611.

Example: They went through a complete sea change in their lifestyle.

Seal of approval

Meaning: A sign of official recognition and approval

Origin: This expression was taken from the idea of wax seals from the Medieval era. This expression was associated with the authenticity of a document.

Example: My dad has given me his seal of approval that I can finally live on my own.

Self-made man

Meaning: Someone who was able to get success through his hard work.

Origin: This expression was taken during the era of Greek kings and how they recognize a person's deeds instead recognizing a person's connections.

Example: Steve Jobs is an example of a self-made man.

Sell like hotcakes

Meaning: Sold out quickly and by large numbers

Origin: This expression originated in the 19th century. It referred to the pancakes that were often sold out in bake sales.

Example: Idol tickets often sell like pancakes.

Set someone's teeth on edge

Meaning: Cause someone to feel intense discomfort or irritation.

Origin: This expression is used in the Bible to describe the unpleasant situation of eating something bitter or sour.

Example: Her mother had set Andy's teeth on edge after hearing her talk about being a lawyer.

Set the record straight

Meaning: Provide accurate information or make an honest statement

Origin: This expression was first cited in the mid-19th century in a citation by The Congressional Globe. It was written as "Mr. BENJAMIN: I think, Mr. President, I have a right to set the record straight upon that point."

Example: To set the record straight, she won the final games three times in a row.

Shake a leg

Meaning: Hurry up, especially in getting out of bed.

Origin: This expression was first used in the 19th century. During this time the British Navy allowed women to be a part of the navy. To boost the morale of the sailors, they would cry "Shake a leg" when everyone in the ship was roused to the first light. Sailors of both genders would raise and shake their legs. If a smooth and female-like leg was presented, the lady was permitted to stay in her bunk until all the men were done dressing and left. This expression is still used even to this day.

Example: Helga should shake a leg if she doesn't want to be late for school.

Shifting sands

Meaning: Something that is constantly changing and keeps the other person feeling uncertain.

Origin: This expression was taken from the idea of sands in an hourglass. It talks about the sand running down which indicates that everything changes with time.

Example: We had no choice but to keep it moving due to the shifting sands.

Shipshape

Meaning: Neat, organized, and clean

Origin: This expression stemmed from the limited space inside the ship. Sailors were obligated to keep everything in their quarters neat and in an orderly fashion. Everything should be in shipshape condition to avoid things from rolling around the ship.

Example: Her bedroom is in shipshape condition.

Shoot the breeze

Meaning: Talking about anything or nothing merely to pass time

Origin: This expression was first cited in the Popular Aviation and Aeronautics Magazine. It was written "We often congregated in unfrequented nooks of the bay to 'shoot the breeze.'

Example: Sara dropped by to shoot the breeze.

Short shrift

Meaning: To give little consideration to

Origin: it was first cited during the 17th century. This expression was taken from the practice of giving shrift to prisoners who were sentenced to be hanged. Shrift is a kind of confession wherein a priest would give the criminal an absolution for all the things he has done. Short shrift is often given to criminals right before they are hanged.

Example: They were given short shrift to submit their homework late.

Shout something from the rooftops

Meaning: Talk about something openly and jubilantly, especially something previously kept secret.

Origin: This idiom was taken from the book of Luke 12:3: stating that 'that which ye have spoken in the ear in closets shall be proclaimed upon the housetops'.

Example: Everyone needs to shout something from the rooftops once in a while. It will make you better after talking about it.

Show someone the door

Meaning: Make someone leave; Lead someone out the door; ask someone to leave

Origin: This expression was taken from a custom of many rich households. Rich families often have butlers to lead the guests into the meeting area until they leave the area. However, throughout the years, this expression became a famous passive-aggressive euphemism whenever they want a person to leave.

Example: Please show Maison the door. I think it's time for him to leave.

Show your true colors

Meaning: Reveal your true intentions or personality.

Origin: This idiomatic expression was both nautical and war-related. During 18th-century naval warfare, battleships were tasked to show their colors. In this context, the flags were considered colors. It was established in the Articles of War in 1757 that captains were required to use their country's flag for their identification. However, this method was also used by many enemies to ensure the victory of their home country. They would often raise a different flag to fool enemies and take them by surprise. Once they were in the firing range, they pulled up their actual flag to take advantage of the enemy.

Example: If you wish to be liked by everyone, then you need to show your true colors.

Side of the angels

Meaning: To agree with the Great and the Good, the orthodox authorities

Origin: This expression was first cited in a speech given by Benjamin Disraeli at Oxford. He used this expression to liken the idea that men and angels are on the side of the Lord and that men are not descendants of apes.

Example: They decided to take the side of the angels on this matter.

Silver lining

Meaning: Something good will happen in the end.

Origin: This expression was coined by John Milton in 1634. He wrote "Was I deceived or did a sable cloud Turn forth her silver lining on the night."

Example: Don't be sad. There's always a silver lining at the end of the storm.

Sink one's teeth into something

Meaning: To enter into a venture with great enthusiasm; to become deeply involved.

Origin: It was cited in 1931 in The Washington Merry-go-round where it was written as: "Stimson actually began to sink his teeth into naval negotiations."

Example: Young business moguls sink their teeth into new products that have never been offered before.

Sink or swim

Meaning: To 'succeed or fail' because of one's own abilities to do so under less-than-perfect circumstances.

Origin: This expression was taken from the English adaptation of the Compleynte until Pite. It was written as 'flete or sinke' which was translated as "float or sink" in English. It was then cited as "sink or swim " in the later years.

Example: You are in control of everything. You can either sink or swim.

Sit below the salt

Meaning: Be of lower social standing or worth.

Origin: This expression used to be a former custom wherein they place a large salt cellar in the middle of a long dining table and that people are seated according to rank.

Example: After the bankruptcy of their company, Robert is now sitting below the salt with his wife.

Sitting on one's hands

Meaning: Withholding the applause; failing to take the appropriate action

Origin: It was first coined in 1927 in a written article by William Smith. In his book Are You Decent?, he wrote "Other performances when they sat on their hands and dared the performer to make 'em like it."

Example: Everyone is sitting on one's hands after her speech on her graduation.

Sixth sense

Meaning: To have an intuition about something

Origin: This phrase was first used in the 1800s. Sixth sense refers to being able to sense something paranormal. It is believed that there is something that can not be detected with the other five senses of your body.

Example: She felt her sixth sense tingling.

Skeleton in the closet

Meaning: A secret that someone is embarrassed about.

Origin: In the past, many grave robbers provided medical schools with skeletons for their lessons. However, because of the 1832 Anatomy Act, medical schools are no longer allowed to keep skeletons in their classrooms. Teachers had to hide skeletons in the closets to avoid confiscation.

Example: In this family, there are tons of skeletons in the closet.

Sleeping with the enemy

Meaning: Someone fraternizing with the enemy

Origin: This phrase was commonly used to describe shady dealings. Although there is no known origin of this phrase, it was used in a movie in 1991 with the same title starring Julia Roberts and Patrick Bergin.

Example: After three shots of chardonnay, I was sleeping with the enemy.

Smell something fishy

Meaning: Feeling suspicious or something is wrong.

Origin: This expression dates back to the early 1800s. In the fish market, one way to tell if the fish is fresh is through its smell. If the fish doesn't give off a foul smell it means it is fresh; if not,then the fish has been in the market for days.

Example: I can smell something fishy from the way they act.

Snow job

Meaning: A very convincing cover up of something.

Origin: This idiom originates from World War II. "Snow job" used to refer to snow under which means to be completely buried. It is also used to refer to the feeling of helplessness or being overwhelmed.

Example: He did a great snow job in fooling everyone in the house.

Someone's just walked over my grave

Meaning: A remark on feeling an involuntary shiver

Origin: This expression was taken from an old wives' tale. This belief states that the person will feel an involuntary shiver in the place where they will be buried.

Example: I think someone just walked over to my grave. I can't stop shivering.

Son of a gun

Meaning: A rogue; usually said to someone in a friendly way

Origin: Centuries ago, the British Navy had allowed women to join sailors on long voyages and live on the ships with them. Some of these women were partners of sailors and some were prostitutes. Thus, pregnancies were normal occurrences. Because of this, sailors created a designated area for babies which was behind the gun. If there were any unplanned pregnancies on the ship where the child's paternity was unknown, the child would be listed as "son of a gun."

Example: You son of a gun! I am so happy to see you!

Sour grapes

Meaning: Comfort is sought in despising what one longs for and cannot have

Origin: It was taken from Aesop's Fable titled the Fox and Grape. In this fable, because of the fox's inability to reach the grapes, he declared them sour.

Example: Maddy was sour graping because Luke is taller than her.

Sparks will fly

Meaning: It is used to refer to angry words or an argument.

Origin: This expression is taken from the word "spark" which is a burning particle thrown off from a fire, but it can also refer to any flash of light.

Example: I can see the sparks will fly if they continue to talk about this absurd topic over and over again.

Spick and span

Meaning: Fresh and unused; neat and clean.

Origin: This expression originated in the 16th century. This expression was used in shipyards. The spick refers to the nail or spike while the span refers or wood chips. If the ship is newly built or clean, you will see the spicks are shiny and rust-free. Aside from that, you will also see some of the span lying around the deck.

Example: Mother had left the kitchen spick and span. Make sure to put everything in the right place.

Spill the beans

Meaning: To leak a secret

Origin: Originated from the Ancient Greek Voting system. In the past, people would vote using colored beans. One red one for yes, a black one for no. If the secret voting results are revealed, then beans are spilled.

Example: Lillian didn't mean to spill the beans.

Spit it out!

Meaning: Hurry up and say it

Origin: This expression is derived from spitting saliva or mucus out of your system. However, this expression indicates the idea of getting rid of something quickly.

Example: Spit it out! I am dying to hear the news.

Squaring the circle

Meaning: Attempting to do the impossible

Origin: This expression was taken during the early 1800's BC when ancient geometers were tasked with constructing a square with the same area as a circle. They were only given a limited number of steps with the use of a compass and straightedge which was something impossible.

Example: The huge number is like squaring the circle.

Stab someone in the back

Meaning: The act of treachery and Betrayal

Origin: This idiom was inspired by the betrayal of Marcus Junius Brutus who betrayed Emperor Gaius Julius Caesar by plunging a knife into his back.

Example: Why did you try to stab someone in the back?

Stand a chance

Meaning: to have a possibility or a hope of success

Origin: This expression was taken from an old phrase from the 1300s. The word "chance" was taken from the French word "cheance". This expression was also related to the Latin word "cadentia" which means "that which falls out."

Example: I know we stand a chance to win this year's cheerleading competition.

Stand on one's own two feet

Meaning: To be independent physically and financially

Origin: This expression was first cited from Britz, of Headquarters, by Marcin Barber in 1910 where it was written as "But there lurked beneath his departmental sense of duty the independence of a man who felt he could always stand on his own two feet, and that he could work alone, if need be, to accomplish the most difficult task."

Example: Jon is trying to stand on his two feet.

Stand one's ground

Meaning: Not retreat or not give up on their current situation.

Origin: The idea behind this idiom was taken from the No Duty to Retreat Law where soldiers are told not to retreat in battle. If a soldier was caught not following, he would be punished with a serious crime.

Example: We are told to stand our ground and wait for the marching orders from the general.

Stand someone in a good stead

Meaning: To be of use to someone, to be someone's advantage.

Origin: This expression was taken from the words good stead. Good stead is often referred to as being in good advantage during the 12th century.

Example: His speaking skills stand him in a good stead when traveling to different places.

Steal one's thunder

Meaning: To use someone else's ideas or inventions to your advantage.

Origin: This idiom came to be when John Dennis complained that someone had stolen his thunder. Dennis, an 18th-century playwright, claimed that he was the first to create a device that makes a thundering sound. He invented this device to be a part of his theater production of Appius and Virginia. However, this method was then copied by another rival production for their version of Macbeth.

Example: She stole my thunder after doing a fantastic job on the last act.

Stick to one's guns

Meaning: To stand by one's belief or conviction

Origin: This expression was first used in print form in the book Life of Samuel Johnson in 1791 by James Boswell. He wrote, "Mrs.Thrale stuck to her gun with great courage in defense of amorous ditties."

Example: We decided to stick to our guns and wait for the outcome.

Stick to your guns

Meaning: Refuse to compromise or change, despite criticism.

Origin: Inspired from the image of a soldier trying to hold his position in enemy fire.

Example: They decided to stick to their guns instead of finding grounds for agreement.

Stick to your last

Meaning: Confine your activities to the area you have personal knowledge of or skill in.

Origin: This expression was taken from the proverb "The cobbler should stick to his last" where the word last referred to the shoemaker's model for shaping and repairing shoes.

Example: It is best that we stick to our last instead of exploring the unknown.

Stop and smell the roses

Meaning: To pause and take a time off from the busy day

Origin: This expression started in the US. There is no clear indication of which year but it was inspired by a story about an avid rose gardener who was told to stop and enjoy her creation.

Example: We all need to stop and smell the roses once in a while.

Straight from the horse's mouth

Meaning: Undeniable. Something you can't contest. A fact

Origin: During ancient times, horses were considered a prized commodity. Many people would often try to lie about the lineage and age of the horses and sell them for a higher price. However, what these swindlers didn't know then is that you can tell the age of the horse by looking at their teeth.

Example: I would like your opinion on this case, straight from the horse's mouth.

Straight shooter

Meaning: Speak honestly and straightforwardly

Origin: This expression was taken from the idea of a bullet going on a straight path. Figuratively, when it was likened to a person, it meant that the person is straightforward and honest just like the bullet.

Example: He was a straight shooter. He will always tell you the truth without sugarcoating anything.

Strike while the iron is hot

Meaning: Take advantage of the opportunities before it is too late

Origin: Inspired by blacksmithing wherein the blacksmith has to strike the heated metal or else it won't be malleable enough to change its shape.

Example: We should strike while the iron is hot. We can make profits out of it.

Strong as an ox

Meaning: Someone strong

Origin: This idiomatic expression comes with several variations. However, this expression talks about someone who is likened to an ox. Throughout the year, the ox is the animal that is always associated with strength and its huge size.

Example: My son is young and strong as an ox.

Stubborn as a mule

Meaning: Very stubborn

Origin: This expression was inspired by mules who have been used as a beast of burden for years. They are known to be unyielding. Most people would consider mules as stubborn beings.

Example: I have never met someone who is as stubborn as a mule.

Suited and booted

Meaning: Formally dressed or well dressed for a certain occasion.

Origin: This expression was first used in India during the Imperial British era. This expression was the most popular Indian way of asking people to get ready for a big event happening.

Example: Colin was all suited and booted for his debut in the orchestra.

Sweep someone off his or her feet

Meaning: Something overwhelming or someone who is literally carried

Origin: This expression made its appearance in 1913 in a Christian novel called The Broken Halo. it was written, "I remember being swept completely off my feet when I first met Jim." This expression has been used ever since."

Example: I am not looking for someone to sweep me off my feet.

T)

Tail between one's legs

Meaning: Someone who is humiliated, hurt his feelings, or damaged due to a clash

Origin: It was derived from a dog's behavior of sticking its tail between his legs whenever he gets scolded by his owner.

Example: I can see their tails between their legs after Sara set the record straight.

Take a leaf out of someone's book

Meaning: To follow another person's example or advice

Origin: This idiom was first coined in the 1800s. It was first used by B.H Malkin when he described the translation done by Gil Blas. He commented on the literal translation from the book. It was like taken from the leaf out of the book.

Example: Her advice was like taken out of someone's book. It was very thorough.

Take a load off

Meaning: To sit down or be comfortable

Origin: This expression was originally "Take a load off your feet". It was first used in the 1930s. Its early reference was taken from The Books of Charles E. Vor Loan, Old Man Curry, and Stories of the Race Track. It was written as "'Sit down, Frank, and take a load off your feet,' said he hospitably."

Example: Come inside, Mira. You can take a load off your feet.

Take five

Meaning: Take a short break; relax.

Origin: This expression is a shorter form of the expression 'a five-minute break.'

Example: We can take five and regroup after.

Take it on the chin

Meaning: Don't shy away from problems; stand up for yourself.

Origin: This expression was originally taken from boxing. It often implies straightness, which can be a critical punch.

Example: Don't be afraid to take it on the chin.

Take someone's name in vain

Meaning: To use someone's name with no respect.

Origin: This idiom was originally one of the Ten Commandments which is 'Thou shalt not take the name of the Lord thy God in vain' (Exodus 20:7).

Example: We should not take someone's name in vain, especially God's.

Take the fall

Meaning: Fall receives blame or punishment, typically in the place of another person.

Origin: This expression was coined from the slang word fall which was associated with the word arrest. It was later extended to mean a term of imprisonment.

Example: Whatever happens on the project, the manager takes the fall.

Take the piss

Meaning: To mock or tease.

Origin: This expression started in the canals of Britain. Before synthetic dyes were created, urine was used to dye wool to recreate the color blue. However, transporting and collecting urine was not lucrative. Many boatmen were forced to lie and claim that they were "taking the wine." However, some people would suspect and ask if these boatmen were "taking the piss."

Example: Edward took a piss at her weak physique.

Take with a pinch of salt

Meaning: To accept something while maintaining a degree of skepticism.

Origin: This expression was first used in1647. This idiom originated from a Roman belief. This belief stated that food was more easily swallowed if taken with a small amount of salt. Pliny the Elder translated an ancient poison antidote with the words 'be taken fasting, plus a grain of salt.' The Romans believed that adding a grain of salt would protect them from lethal poisoning.

Example: You need to take the information with a pinch of salt.

Take your hat off (or raise your hat)

Meaning: Talk about your admiration for someone

Origin: The image here is of the gesture of briefly removing your hat as a mark of courtesy or respect to someone.

Example: I think he should take off his hat for Michael Jordan.

Taken aback

Meaning: Startled or surprised by a sudden change.

Origin: This naval expression is often used in sailing. When you say 'back' it means that the ship is facing towards the rear and the sails are flat against the mast. A sudden wind change can slow the ship down and sometimes drive the ship backward. Hence, the ship was "taken to aback"

Example: I was taken aback after she told me the news.

Taste of one's own medicine

Meaning: You experience what you have given to others.

Origin: Thesis expression was derived from bad-tasting medicine. However, it was then used figuratively in 1874. It was written in a paper about free religion. It was written as a letter to the editor stating: ...in case of uproarious persistence on their part to inculcate their dangerous 'views,' should lock up their meeting-houses, and send the preachers to jail; that would be giving the Doctor a taste of his own medicine..."

Example: She got a taste of her own medicine when she got swindled back.

Tell it to the marines

Meaning: I don't believe you

Origin: This expression was first coined during the mid-1600s when the rivalry between the marines and sailors came to be. Sailors believe that many marines are stupid due to their limited experience in the sea, failing to see the difference in their skillsets in sea navigation. The expression was born to insult the marines.

Example: You can tell it to the marines!

Test the waters

Meaning: Trying something new but in a cautious manner.

Origin: This expression was first used in July 1922. It was used as a printed reference from a Washington newspaper stating "The Washington State Press Association seems to be embarking upon an uncharted sea in planning an all-newspaper program for its thirty-fifth annual convention at Pullman, July 14-15-16. But editors are anxious to test the waters."

Example: We decided to test the waters on some of the new products.

That way madness lies

Meaning: It is ill-advised to pursue a particular course of action as it will cause distress or anxiety.

Origin: This expression was taken from the play called King Lear where Lear shies away from contemplating the ingratitude of his own daughters.

Example: She said that it was "that way madness lies", but still went for it.

That's the ticket!

Meaning: What a person exactly needed

Origin: This idiom dates back to the early 19th century. This expression first appeared in print in 1838. This expression was written in Samuel Slick of Slickville by Thomas Haliburton. He wrote, "They ought to be hanged, sir, (that's the ticket, and he'd whop the leader).". Different variations have been used since then.

Example: That's the ticket that I have been looking for!

That's the way the ball bounces

Meaning: That is how things happen; there is nothing one can do to change it.

Origin: It was first cited in a song on the RCA Victor record label entitled 'That's the Way the Big Ball Bounces.

Example: She was resigned to her fate. That's the way the ball bounces.

The answer's a lemon

Meaning: The response or outcome is unsatisfactory.

Origin: The word "lemon" is used to represent something bad and unsatisfactory. This could be because lemons tend to be the least valuable symbol when playing on the slot machine.

Example: Her answer's a lemon. I don't think we did well on this project.

The ball's in your court

Meaning: It's your turn to make a move

Origin: Inspired by tennis. People would use the expression when they see the ball on the other side of the net.

Example: It is up to you to decide. The ball is in your court.

The best thing since sliced bread

Meaning: A really good invention.

It may have originated in the 1930s when the Continental Baking Company introduced the first pre-sliced loaf 'Wonder Bread'. The advertising campaign promoting the innovative product soon appeared in households everywhere.

Example: Cryptocurrency is the best thing since sliced bread.

The brains behind

Meaning: The person who made and organized the successful plan.

Origin: This idiom was first inspired by the idiom "the brain." This expression is used to refer to intelligence. Hence, the expression "the brains behind" refers to the smart person behind the succession plan.

Example: The brains behind Project X have been awarded for their outstanding work.

The buck stops here

Meaning: The responsibility for a situation or a problem with somebody.

Origin: This expression was taken from another idiom "Pass the buck" which means that it was passing the responsibility to another person. This expression became popular after US President Harry S. Truman often used this phrase in many of his speeches.

Example: I cannot keep on blaming the doctor who did my operation; the buck stops with me as a patient.

The chips are down

Meaning: The situation has reached a crisis point; the moment of truth, of trial, of testing has come

Origin: It was first coined in gambling. When they say chips are down it means that all bets are placed and everyone is just waiting for the game to finish.

Example: The chips are down, it's time to give them the result.

The cut of his/her jib

Meaning: The general appearance of one person

Origin: A jib is a type of sail. At one time countries would display their own unique jibs, allowing outsiders to instantly know the ship's origin, and form an impression of it.

Example: Nelly could easily tell from the cut of her jib that everything she wore is expensive.

The devil to pay

Meaning: Serious trouble to be expected.

Origin: This expression refers to the bargain between magicians and devils. It is often equated with mortals gaining extraordinary power or wealth in return.

Example: She knows that there'll be a devil to pay.

The devil you know

Meaning: Something or someone bad that you are familiar with and have accommodated yourself to or can cope with.

Origin: This expression was derived from the proverb 'Better the devil you know than the one you don't'.

Example: It is better to go through hardships than make a deal with the devil you know.

The die is cast

Meaning: An event has happened or a decision has been taken that cannot be changed.

Origin: This expression was first coined as Julius Caesar's remark as he was about to cross the river Rubicon making him technically an invader to Italy.

Example: The die is cast, there is nothing we can do about it.

The eye of a needle

Meaning: A very small opening or space (used to emphasize the impossibility of a projected endeavor).

Origin: This idiom is taken from Matthew 19:24: 'It is easier for a camel to go through the eye of a needle, than for a rich man to enter the kingdom of "God."

Example: We were able to pass through the eye of a needle.

The flavor of the month

Meaning: Something temporarily in fashion

Origin: This idiomatic expression was taken from an American ice cream parlor in the 1950s. It was used to encourage customers to try out some of their new flavors.

Example: Sadly, she is Danny's flavor of the month.

The grass is always greener

Meaning: Other people's lives or situations always seem better than your own.

Origin: This expression was a shortened form of the proverb 'the grass is always greener on the other side of the fence' which is often associated with dissatisfaction with one's current disposition.

Example: The grass is always greener on the other side of the road, if you want to start anew in another country.

The heart is in the right place

Meaning: The intention is proper and that the person is a good individual

Origin: This was first used in a missionary publication in 1833. It was quoted by the Church Missionary Society, London, in the February issue: "A well-educated Hindu Christian is worth a great deal to our work if his heart is in the right place, but such is rare."

Example: Her heart was in the right place when she decided to start a rescue center.

The jig is up

Meaning: The scheme or deception is revealed or foiled.

Origin: In the late 16th century, the word 'jig' was used to refer to "jest" or "trick." However, the expression was first coined around the late 18th century in the USA.

Example: They have no choice but to reveal that the jig is up.

The joker in the pack

Meaning: A person or factor likely to have an unpredictable effect on events.

Origin: In a pack of cards, a joker card comes as an extra card that does not belong to any of the suits. It also bears the drawing of a jester. In some card games, like poker, the jester plays an important role.

Example: Her appearance was the joker in the pack. Unexpectedly, she changed the outcome of the game.

The lion's share

Meaning: the larger part

Origin: This idiom was originally from Aesop's Fables. In this fable, a lion and three other animals hunted a stage. They were supposed to share the hunt equally. However, the lion claimed that he should have three portions of the hunt because he was the leader, the strongest, and courageous among them. The other animals should share the fourth portion. He threatened to kill them if they tried to touch his portions.

Example: Grizelda has the lion's share because she owns the majority of the stocks.

The Midas touch

Meaning: The ability to make money out of anything that you undertake.

Origin: This expression was inspired by the legend of King Midas of Phrygia who was given the power to turn everything he touched into gold.

Example: Dane has that Midas touch. He can make every business successful.

The middle of nowhere

Meaning: Somewhere very remote and isolated.

Origin: This expression was often used as something derogative of rural life. From an urban perspective, the rural area is considered "the middle of nowhere" due to the lack of urban features.

Example: Sadly, I am stuck in the middle of nowhere in this town.

The old Adam

Meaning: The evil side of human nature.

Origin: This expression is used to express the "old Adam" who was the first man in the Garden of Eden. He was compared to the "Second Adam" which referred to Jesus Christ.

Example. Dan is indeed an Old Adam.

The one that got away

Meaning: Something desirable that has eluded capture

Origin: Inspired by the angler's traditional way of catching a large fish that managed to escape after almost being caught.

Example: This angler fish was the one that got away.

The pecking order

Meaning: The social hierarchy which dictates one's relationship to those above and below one

Origin: Originated in the chicken coop where hens determine their dominance by pecking one another.

Example: My parrot, Jinx, had set the pecking order between the birds in my flock.

The penny dropped

Meaning: The joke, remark, or point of the argument has suddenly been grasped

Origin: This expression was inspired by the slot machines found in piers and penny arcades. These machines were often not working until the penny was dropped. This expression is used figuratively when a person doesn't understand the joke after hearing it for the first time.

Example: It was only until the penny dropped that she understood the joke.

The pot calling the kettle black

Meaning: Someone who is guilty of doing something they are accused of.

Origin: This idiom was first used during the Medieval Period when pots and kettles were the most used kitchen tools. During this era, pots and kettles would often get blackened by the soot from the open fire. This phrase was first used in literary form in Thomas Shelton's translation of the Spanish novel "Don Quixote. " In the book, Don Quixote exclaimed, "You are like what is said that the frying-pan said to the kettle, 'Avant, black-browes'."

Example: I am not saying that this is not a situation for the pot calling the kettle black, but Mila's actions tell me otherwise.

The proof is in the pudding

Meaning: Achieving the goal regardless of the method

Origin: During the 16th century, the first pudding was invented. However, it took a long time to perfect the pudding's taste and texture. People used several methods on how to create the pudding until they were able to attain the right taste and texture.

Example: She did well regardless of the method. The proof is in the pudding.

The scales fall from someone's eyes

Meaning: No longer deceived.

Origin: In the Bible, this expression described how St Paul, blinded by his vision on the road to Damascus, received his sight back at the hand of God (Acts 9:18).

Example: After the scales fell from my eyes, everything seemed to be clearer.

The tip of an (or the) iceberg

Meaning: The small perceptible part of a much larger situation or problem which remains hidden.

Origin: This phrase refers to the fact that only about one-fifth of the mass of an iceberg is visible above the surface of the sea.

Example: The tip of the iceberg of this situation is when he stole several million without us knowing.

The upper crust

Meaning: The aristocracy and upper classes.

Origin: Originally, this expression was inspired by the nickname Mrs. Upper Crust. Mrs. Upper Crust was a person who assumed superiority among others.

Example: People in the upper crust live in luxurious mansions and cars.

The vale of years

Meaning: The declining years of a person's life; old age.

Origin: An expression created from Shakespeare's Othello wherein it said 'for I am declin'd into the vale of years.'

Example: Now that I am in the vale of years, it is time for me to retire.

The writing is on the wall

Meaning: Certain results have become inevitable.

Origin: This phrase was originally taken from the Bible. This referred to the warning of Belshazzar's final judgment because of his wicked ways.

Example. As clear as the writing on the wall, the results shown are final.

There is no rose without a thorn

Meaning: Regardless of how good the situation is, there is always trouble that comes with it.

Origin: This idiom was first recorded in a poem in the 15th century. It was first seen in the work of John Lydgate (1370-1451) where he wrote: 'There is no rose...in the garden, but there be sum thorne'.

Example: Life is never happy if there is no rose without a thorn.

There's (or here's) the rub

Meaning: The crucial part of the problem.

Origin: This expression came from Shakespeare's Hamlet: 'To sleep: perchance to dream: ay, there's the rub; For in that sleep of death what dreams may come when we have shuffled off this mortal coil, Must give us pause.' In the game of bowls, a rub is an impediment that prevents a bowl from running smoothly.

Example: There's a rub on the story. How are we going to tell them the truth?

There's no time like the present

Meaning: To stop procrastinating on your duties.

Origin: This idiom was first used in printed form in the magazine The Theosophist Volume XXX. it was printed as " "...even as it is said, what was the Present has become Past, and bears a relation to another point in Future Time to the negation of the Present. Yet there is no time like the present. The whole gist of life to the Occultist is merged in it."

Example: Today is a great time to hustle. There is no time like the present.

Things that go bump in the night

Meaning: Ghosts; supernatural beings.

Origin: Originally this expression was taken from The Cornish or West Country Litany, starting 'From ghoulies and ghosties and long-leggety beasties And things that go bump in the night, Good Lord deliver us!' Since then, this expression was used comically to describe nocturnal disturbances of all sorts.

Example: They say there are tons of things that go bump in the night in this house. Now, I am scared.

Things went south

Meaning: Something went wrong at some point

Origin: The word south means on the lower part or going down. Most people associate this idea with business and stock. If the charts are going down, then it means something is wrong.

Example: Things went south before we were able to solve the situation.

Thinking outside the box

Meaning: Thinking from another perspective

Origin: This expression was first used in the UK by Edward de Bono as "Lateral Thinking". However, it was only then in Sam Loyd's Cyclopedia of 5000 Puzzles, Tricks, and Conundrums that the actual definition of the box came to be.

Example: Thinking outside the box can help you find the most unconventional solutions to your problems.

Third time lucky

Meaning: After failing twice to accomplish something, the third attempt may be successful.

Origin: This expression was taken from the idiomatic expression "third time's the charm."

Example. Indeed, I am third time lucky! Finally clipped my dog's nails after two failing attempts.

Through thick and thin

Meaning: No matter how difficult the situation

Origin: This expression was taken from sailors simply hoisting the thick and thin ropes no matter what the circumstance is.

Example: I will always help you, through thick and thin.

Throw a curveball

Meaning: Misleading someone by placing unexpected problems along their way.

Origin: This expression was inspired by baseball. Pitchers throw curveballs to confuse the batter.

Example: You can throw a curveball on several parts of the game.

Throw cold water on

Meaning: To discourage the advancement of a certain long-awaited situation

Origin: This expression was first used by Plateaus who used the expression to mean slander. However, the meaning of the expression changed throughout the 19th century. In its printed reference in 1861 where George Eliot's Silas Marner where he wrote "It was to be hoped that Mr. Godfrey would not go to Tarley and throw cold water on what Mr. Snell said there, and so prevent the justice from drawing up a warrant."

Example: She doesn't want to throw cold water on me, but she doesn't have a choice at all.

Throw good money after bad

Meaning: Wasting money on a losing proposition

Origin: It was first used during the mid-20th century. It was first cited in a play titled After the Fall by Arthur Miller in 1964.

Example: We shouldn't throw good money after the bad, especially this time around.

Throw someone to the lions

Meaning: Cause someone to be in an extremely dangerous or unpleasant situation.

Origin: It was taken from the Roman practices where Christians and other religious and political dissidents were thrown into the arena full of lions.

Example: Tina threw everyone to the lions because she knew that cheating on the test was wrong.

Thumbs up (or down)

Meaning: An indication of satisfaction or approval (or of rejection or failure).

Origin: This expression dates back to ancient Rome to express an approval or disapproval of spectators. Thumbs down mean that the gladiator has done well and should be saved while the thumbs up to call for his death.

Example: I am going to give this book a thumbs up for having the best plot.

Tick off

Meaning: to make a mark next to items on a list that have been completed; to make someone angry or offended

Origin: This idiom comes with several uses. However, it dates back to the 1800s. It was used to describe a small mark or dot that indicates a sale. The evolution of this definition started in the early 1900s which was cited by Wilfred Owen's Collected letters. Tick off was then defined as getting angry or offended.

Example: I see many of the objectives are ticked off; you are almost done with the experiment.

Tide you over

Meaning: To supply someone with something they need for a short period.

Origin: In the era of exploration, sailors would often propel the ship with the tide when there was no wind. The tide also helped lift the ship away from obstructions like coral reefs and sandbars. This phrase was first used by Captain John Smith in his book A Sea Gramma in 1627. He wrote that "To tide over to a place, is to go out with the Tide of ebb or flood, and stop the contrary by anchoring till the next Tide." Since then, this expression has been used figuratively.

Example: I bought everything you need to tide you over during the whole duration of the quarantine.

Tie the knot

Meaning: To take one's marriage vows

Origins: This expression was taken from the idea of tying knots during ancient marriage rituals. In many marriage practices, the husband and wife are often tied to a garment that symbolizes their marriage.

Example: They decided that it was time to tie the knot.

Tight as a tick

Meaning: Extremely drunk.

Origin: This expression was inspired by blood-sucking insects during the 17th century. These insects would gorge themselves until they were full. In modern times, this expression is likened to drunk people who would drink until they are full.

Example: Chester was tight as a tick after drinking all the wine in the cellar.

Tighten your belt

Meaning: To economize

Origin: This expression was inspired by the idea of moving the buckle from one hole to another after the man loses weight. This expression was one of the popular expressions during the economic depression in the 1930s.

Example. Money is tight right now, so we need to tighten our belts a bit.

Till the cows come home

Meaning: For a long indefinite and unpredictable time.

Origin: Dates back to the pastoral era when cows and other cattle would take a long time to graze one area.

Example: Till the cows come home, let's just wait for Papa to finish his journey.

Till/to kingdom come

Meaning: Forever; to death

Origin: This expression was taken from the Bible in Matthew 6:10 when he talked about the Lord's Prayer.

Example: We have to fight till the Kingdom comes.

To bandy something about

Meaning: To spread unfavorable or untrue ideas

Origin: This expression was inspired by the French word "bander" which was an early form of the tennis game. However, this expression evolved through time. Instead of referring to a sport, this expression refers to the idea of arguing with someone.

Example: Many supporters have decided to bandy about the opposing candidate.

To bank on something

Meaning: To count or depend on something

Origin: This expression was inspired by the early banking system in Medieval Venice. During these times, people would use benches called "banco" in the main square. These bankers would change and lend money in different currencies.

Example: Should we bank on Melisa to help us with this predicament?

To be in someone's black books

Meaning: To be out of favor with someone, to be in disgrace

Origin: The Black book or black books used to be an expression that refers to the reports made on monastic hilding and allegations of corruption inside the Church. The said black book was compiled by Henry VII as he sought information to help him sever the ties between his kingdom and the Papal Authority.

Example: I don't want to be in Anastacia's black books if I were you.

To be left high and dry

Meaning: Left out of place; Left stranded

Origin: This nautical phrase is used to describe a ship that was left grounded after it was washed out of the tide.

Example: I was left high and dry at a party that I am not comfortable with.

To be on the cards

Meaning: To be possible, to be likely to happen

Origin: This expression was coined during the 19th century when the practice of fortune-telling and Tarot Card readings came to be.

Example: It was to be on the cards that our team will become the champion for this season.

To be taken to the cleaners

Meaning: To lose all one's money, to be ruined

Origin: This expression started during the last century. The expression "clean out" used to mean stripping everything of value, including gambling money. This expression is another variation of the words "clean out."

Example: Everything has to be taken to the cleaners, nothing should be left.

To bear down

Meaning: Exert effort on a person using authority and swift action

Origin: Stems from naval battles where an attacking ship will bear down on another enemy ship. They would use the wind to increase their maneuverability and deliver firepower.

Example: The cops have to bear down on the suspect to keep him from attempting to escape again.

To bell the cat

Meaning: To undertake a difficult mission at great personal risk

Origin: This idiom originated from the ancient fable that is related by Langland to Piers Plowman in 1377. It talks about a colony of mice who tried to bell the cat that has been terrorizing their territory. However, as much as they want to bell the cat, the obvious question was "Who will bell the cat?" In Scottish history, there was another similar situation to the fable. The members of the court of James III were all wary of the new architect named Cochran. The nobles believed that he was the King's new favorite and that they needed to get rid of him. However, they were also left with the question "Who will bell the cat?" It was the Earl of Angus, Archibald Angus who volunteered to bell the cat. He seized Cochran and had him hanged over the bridge of Lauder. His act of belling the cat earned him the nickname "Bell-the-Cat" Douglas

Example: Sharon has to bell the cat before she becomes a full-pledge officer.

To blackball

Meaning: To exclude someone from a social group or club

Origin: This expression was first coined during the 18th century when applicants would choose new members for their exclusive clubs. They would use a white ball or a black ball in an urn. A white ball would signify a yes while a black ball would signify a no.

Example: They had to blackball Mark in their club due to bad behavior.

To blacklist

Meaning: To list the name of someone contravening rules or conventions; to ostracize

Origin: During the reign of Charles II, he had created a list of implicated people who were behind the death and execution of his father Charles I.

Example: She had to blacklist some people on her phone.

To boot

Meaning: In addition, as well

Origin: In the past, the word Boot didn't always refer to a pair of boots, rather it was referred to as "profit" or "advantage."

Example: To boot, make sure to submit your homework on time.

To chip in

Meaning: To contribute; to interrupt

Origin: originally, this phrase was taken from poker where players have to place their chips in the pot. These chips are the sum of the amount that the player will win after the game.

Example: I can chip in some information that you need to know about the situation.

To climb on the bandwagon

Meaning: To support a plan or cause for personal profit or advantage

Origin: This expression was inspired by the political rallies in the past, especially in the southern part of the US. Electoral candidates would hire a horse-drawn wagon with a musical band and parade all over town. This was their way of telling the people that they are running for political office.

Example: They decided to climb on the bandwagon using the current trends in Tik Tok.

To cross one's fingers

Meaning: To be hoping for luck or a happy outcome

Origin: This expression was said to be the easiest way to make a sign of a cross to protect oneself from possible harm. Many people believe that this expression was taken from the black slave population.

Example: She crossed her fingers hoping that she passed the interview.

To cry wolf

Meaning: To complain when there's nothing actually wrong; to lie or pull a prank

Origin: The origin of this idiom comes from "Aesop's Fables". Specifically, "to cry wolf" came from the fable "The Shepherd Boy and the Wolf". To summarize, the boy pulled a prank on the shepherds by shouting "wolf". Shepherds came running to protect their herd only to find out that they had been pranked. Eventually, the real wolf came and attacked the herd. The boy cried out "Wolf!" but the shepherds no longer believed him. The moral, related to Aesop, was that "a liar will not be believed, even when he speaks the truth".

Example: No matter how hard the job is, we must be careful not to cry wolf.

To cut no ice with someone

Meaning: To make no impression upon someone, to be powerless to influence someone

Origin: Originated during the late 19th century. It was inspired by ice skating. A person can't move gracefully on ice if the blades are not keen and cut. Blunt blades don't make a good impression on ice.

Example: She made sure that would cut no ice with anyone in the group.

To cut to the quick

Meaning: To cause someone deep emotional hurt

Origin: The word "quick" came from the Old English word "wicu" which means living. It also refers to the most sensitive flesh in the body that is protected by the fingernails and toenails. Hence, when this area gets a small cut, it's more painful compared to the other parts of the body.

Example: They were cut to the quick by their guilt.

To double cross

Meaning: A deliberate betrayal, usually by a previous partner; a violation of a promise

Origin: Dating back to the 18th century when London Bounty Hunter Jonathan Wild would hunt criminals. Wild would usually keep important information about all the criminals in London. He would mark a cross on their name. If the criminal had two crosses on their name, he would be then executed by Wild.

Example: It was not her purpose to double-cross them.

To draw a blank

Meaning: Unsuccessful; Failed attempts.

Origin: To draw a blank refers to the blank lottery tickets that can be drawn during numbered lottery games.

Example: She had been drawing blanks while solving the puzzle.

To enter the lion's den

Meaning: To undergo an extreme test, to face overwhelming opposition

Origin: This expression was inspired by the idea that lions are the bravest and most ferocious beasts in the world, entering their death might be fatal.

Example: The mid-term test was like entering the lion's den.

To fiddle while Rome burns

Meaning: to be occupied with small things when a crisis is happening.

Origin: The origin of this idiom started in AD64 with Emperor Nero. To get the same impression of what happened in Troy, he set Rome on fire while playing with his lyre. Rome burned for 6 days and 7 days. Nero denied the claims of burning Rome. He blamed the Christians and had them persecuted.

Example: People just sat while Rome burned between Josh and Catalina.

To get cold feet

Meaning: Disheartened, discourage

Origin: Originally taken from Medieval Europe where soldiers could no longer fight due to frostbite.

Example: Don't get cold feet, you will be able to solve this mystery.

To get into a scrape

Meaning: To get into an embarrassing situation, usually as a result of one's own carelessness

Origin: This expression was taken from a story of Frances Tucker who was killed by a stag's scrape and met its fury in Powderham Park.

Example: In what situation do we usually get into a scrape?

To get/give someone a break

Meaning: To get/be given a good opportunity; to be let off

Origin: Originally, this expression was used to be underworld slang. This expression was used by criminal communities in the 19th century. The break is a collection or a whip around made for a felon who was released from jail.

Example: It has been a long day, please give me a break!

To go cold turkey

Meaning: To come off (hard) drugs abruptly, rather than gradually and more easily

Origin: This expression is commonly associated with drug use. However, in olden times, this expression was used to signify a plain dish served with no garnishes or sauces. In the current times, cold turkey is likened to the withdrawal method of drug use which is basic and straightforward.

Example: She went cold turkey after learning the dangers of excessive drinking of alcohol.

To go to the wall

Meaning: To make every possible effort to achieve something, to win, etc.

Origin: This expression dated back to England during the Medieval times when going to church was compulsory. Churches then did not have seats, hence people were forced to sit on the wall or stand during the masses. Hence, the expression "the weakest go to the wall".

Example: Players want to go to the wall and bring home the trophy.

To hang fire

Meaning: To be pending, delayed

Origin: This expression was taken from the idea of old firearms. In the past, the main charge of the gun took a long time to ignite which makes the gun a hanging fire.

Example: Phase one is done, let's hang fire for now and wait for their approval.

To have someone over a barrel

Meaning: Helpless; at someone's mercy

Origin: Over the barrel is a maritime practice that is done by many sailors. After saving a drowning sailor, they would put him on his stomach over the barrel. This way, they can empty the water in their lungs. Sailors that were put over the barrel were often described as helpless.

Example: To have someone over the barrel is not an ideal situation.

To hit rock bottom

Meaning: To reach the lowest point in your life

Origin: This naval idiom stemmed from the situation when a ship hit the bottom of the ocean and got stuck between the rocks.

Example: The death of her mother caused her to hit rock bottom.

To hold the fort

Meaning: To take care of things, take over briefly

Origin: This expression was first used during the American Civil War. It was inspired by General William Tecumseh Sherman when he sent the message to Union General John Murrage Corse saying "Hold the fort, I am coming."

Example: Please hold the fort for me while I run errands for the boss.

To live on a shoestring

Meaning: To manage on very little money

Origin: This phrase originated in the 1800s. It was inspired by the idea that people with less money can only afford a shoelace as the most expensive thing.

Example: Before payday comes, we all try to live on shoestrings.

To make (both) ends meet

Meaning: To live within one's means

Origin: This expression was taken from the 17th century when people found it hard to balance their income with their expenditures. But it was often used in accountancy. "Meet" was referred to as "equal" and the word "end" refers to the accounting year.

Example: Mara has to make both ends meet just to make sure everyone is well-provided.

To move the goalposts

Meaning: To change the rules

Origin: This expression is a sports idiom that was adopted in the real world. It means that changing the rules can change the outcome of a certain situation.

Example: We may be the host school, but we should never move the goalposts to our advantage.

To nip something in the bud

Meaning: To prevent a bad habit from starting

Origin: This idiom has emphasized the idea of correcting a habit before it becomes worse in later years. This idea was likened to a gardener and a bud. Many gardeners don't hesitate to pinch buds to encourage them to grow stronger in the future.

Example: Parents often nip the bad actions in the bud before it becomes a habit.

To paint the town red

Meaning: To go out and enjoy oneself in a flamboyant or over the top manner.

Origin: The Marquis of Warefor got drunk and painted some of the town's buildings red. It has been the talk of the town since then.

Example: Today is a day to celebrate! Let's go out and paint the town red.

To pass the buck

Meaning: Passing the responsibility to someone else

Origin: The word "buck" is a poker term that refers to markers placed in front of the players. This marker will determine whose turn it is to deal with. The dealer will then declare the first stake and has the power to choose whether or not they will pass the marker. Hence, the idiom "to pass the buck."

Example: They are willing to pass the buck after the company has gone bankrupt.

To pay for the nail

Meaning: To make a prompt cash payment

Origin: This expression was taken from an old medieval practice on how payments were being made. In the past, buyers would place their payments in pillar-like counters called nails. This was their method to attest their proof of bargain.

Example: She bought a new car today. She decided to pay for the nail.

To pay through the nose

Meaning: To pay an exorbitant price for something

Origin: This expression was derived from a certain practice in Ireland when the Danes had successfully invaded them. People were asked to pay a hefty sum of tax. If they refused to pay, their nose was slit in half. In the modern time, this expression is also associated with Rhinoplasty.

Example: We have to pay through the nose just to get the best flight tickets going to Hawaii.

To play/wreak havoc

Meaning: to devastate, destroy, spoil

Origin: Originally, the word Havoc was borrowed from an old French word "havot". The word "havot" means plunder.

Example: He was planning to wreak havoc on the current government.

To pour oil on troubled waters

Meaning: To soothe a quarrel, to calm a heated argument

Origin: This expression was taken from a miracle performed by Bishop Aidan. During the voyage of escorting the bride of King Oswy, the bishop prophesied an approaching storm. To avoid the storm, he poured a phial of holy water into the ocean.

Example: My mother has to pour oil on troubled waters whenever my sisters are quarreling.

To put a spoke in someone's wheel

Meaning: Purposely hinder someone's plans or success

Origin: This expression was inspired by the wheels of the cart that are connected to a bar of wood called a spoke. The spoke is often used to help regulate the speed of the cartwheel.

Example: Someone put a spoke in Ginny's wheel because they thought she would give up halfway.

To put one's foot in one's mouth

Meaning: To say something accidentally that could cause offense

Origin: This expression is used to refer to people saying something wrong. However, this expression was continually used to accuse Church people of doing this act as a habit in the past.

Example: We should warn Dana not to put her foot in her mouth. She might accidentally offend Rosey.

To read the riot act

Meaning: Reprimand or to call out a person who is misbehaving.

Origin: It dates back to the 1800s. During this time, Jacobites were known to use violence to replace the people on the throne. Because of this, the royals were forced to create the riot act to avoid this violent uprising caused by the Jacobites.

Example: You need to read the riot act and start acting properly in the class.

To ring a bell

Meaning: To remind someone of something, to jog someone's memory (of a shared experience)

Origin: There were several speculations behind this expression. However, the closest one would be coined by Funk (1955). To ring a bell is inspired by nostalgic school bells and church bells

Example: Does this situation ring a bell to you? Just like what happened in high school.

To rub salt in the wound

Meaning: Intentionally increase someone's pain, discomfort

Origin: Based on the idea that wounds need to be re-opened and cleaned before they fully heal. In order to do so, salt is rubbed into the wounds.

Example: Tony had rubbed salt into my wound. I am both physically and emotionally hurt.

To save one's bacon

Meaning: To escape injury or difficulty; to rescue someone from trouble

Origin: This expression was originally the allusion to protecting or securing the bacon stored for the winter season, especially in a household full of dogs.

Example: My dog just saved my bacon after the accident.

To see a man about a dog

Meaning: Disguise the purpose of one's business

Origin: This expression was coined from the play titled Flying Scud by Dion Boucicault. In this play, the character uses this strategy to get away from a tricky situation.

Example: To see a man about a dog, they were not able to notice that there was something.

To sell someone down the river

Meaning: To put someone in a difficult or dangerous situation by not acting as you had promised to act, usually in order to win an advantage for yourself

Origin: This expression was taken during the 19th century Slave Trade in the Southern part of the US. Importing slaves was already illegal around this time. However, there were still some internal slaves happening, especially down the Mississippi River.

Example: He sold her down the river and told the police that she was the mastermind behind the crime.

To set off on the right/wrong foot

Meaning: To begin something well/badly

Origin: In Roman beliefs, the left foot is considered the "wrong foot". In olden times, the left is considered "evil" and the gods are guiding the "right" to protect you from the left. Petronius even exhorted his fellow Romans to enter a house with their right foot and that they should also leave the house with their right foot. Carrying the bride to the threshold is another tradition that stems from this Roman belief. The husband has to carry the wife over the threshold to avoid starting their new life on the wrong foot.

Example: The princesses set off on the wrong foot because of a petty misunderstanding.

To show the white feather

Meaning: To show cowardice

Origin: This expression was taken from cock-pit. In the past, cocks that were considered pure didn't have white feathers on them. Cocks with white feathers are considered underbred, and come with high defects from its breeding.

Example: He noticed that his enemy was showing the white feather, so he decided to punch him square in the face.

To sign the pledge

Meaning: To give up alcohol

Origin: This expression was popularized during the 19th century when people of different statuses would raise their glass of strong liquor and publicly declare their resolve by.signing a certain pledge not to drink it again.

Example: One of the members refused to sign the pledge.

To start from scratch

Meaning: To start from the beginning without any advantage or help.

Origin: The scratch used to mean the starting point of the race. It was a line etched into the ground. Figuratively, it was often used by many sportsmen then and now. They need to start from the beginning of the race without any help or a handicap system to back them up.

Example: If you want to learn how to cook, then you need to start from scratch.

To take the bull by the horns

Meaning: To face up to difficulty with boldness

Origin: This expression stems from the Spanish Bull-fighting. Bulls were tormented and angered by the banderilleros. They would pierce the bull's neck with darts until its head droops. It makes it easier for the matador to play with his cape in the ring. Sometimes, the matador would take the bull by its horns before killing it.

Example: You need to take the bull by the horns if you wish to succeed in life.

To take the cake

Meaning: To deserve honor or merit; to be outrageous

Origin: This idiomatic expression came with several origins in the past. One of them was taken during the late 19th century. Black slaves were used as a form of amusement in many Southern US Plantations. The white slave-owners would often admire cries from the black slaves. A judge came and said 'That takes the cake' which was synonymous with the grand prize.'

Example: Mirabella takes the cake for the best interior design.

To talk gibberish

Meaning: To talk unintelligibly or in an obscure and meaningless way

Origin: The word "gibberish" is originally from the word "Geber", an Arabian Alchemist who liked to create his own terminology to avoid people copying his work.

Example: I can hear my sister talk gibberish to her dog.

To the letter

Meaning: With adherence to every detail.

Origin: It was taken from the French phrase "au pied de la lettre" translated as "to the letter." This expression has been used since the late 18th century.

Example: Make sure that you follow everything to the letter.

To the manner born

Meaning: Naturally at ease in a specified way of life, job, or situation.

Origin: Taken from Shakespeare's Hamlet where he wrote 'though I am native here And to the manner born.'

Example: I am a farmer and to the manner born.

To the moon and back

Meaning: Greater than this outsized distance

Origin: This expression was taken from the children's book called Guess How Much I Love You by Sam McBratney. This expression was inspired by the story of two plush rabbits. A father and son boasted how much they love each other. The father declared that he loved his son to the moon and back.

Example: You have my support to the moon and back.

To throw down the gauntlet

Meaning: To challenge someone

Origin: This expression was inspired by an old practice during the Medieval era where knights would challenge each other by throwing down the gauntlet to their opponent.

Example: Mila will throw down the gauntlet on Shana for the next presidential race.

To throw up/in the sponge

Meaning: To give up, to admit defeat

Origin: This expression was taken from boxing. If a boxer is defeated in a match, his corner will toss up the sponge that was used to freshen the fighter during the fight. This is also similar to throwing in the towel in a match.

Example: We decided to throw up the sponge. It seems we can't find the answer to this riddle.

To turn the other cheek

Meaning: The attitude of forgiving a person for doing something bad to you

Origin: This is a phrase from the Bible. In Matthew 5:39 Jesus exhorts his followers with these words: 'But I say unto you, That ye resist not evil: but whosoever shall smite thee on thy right cheek, turn to him the other also.'

Example: Let God help you turn the other cheek.

To write like an angel

Meaning: To have beautiful handwriting; to be a gifted writer of prose or poetry

Origin: This idiom was written and created by Isaac D'Israeli in his book Curiosities of Literature. He likened a calligrapher to someone who writes like an angel.

Example: A calligrapher writes like an angel.

Toe the line

Meaning: To submit to authority, regulations, etc

Origin: This expression was taken from track and field races. Players would put their toes on the starting line and wait for the gun to signal the start of the race.

Example: Students love to toe the lines with their teachers.

Tongue in cheek

Meaning: Something said in humor, but with an act of being serious

Origin: This expression is inspired by the literal facial expression created when you say something as a joke.

Example: She was a cheeky little thing, she had her tongue in her cheek when she told me the joke.

Too close for comfort

Meaning: To be very close to something dangerous or unwelcoming

Origin: This expression was first used in the early 1800s. It was first cited in The New Monthly Magazine and Literary Journal, United Kingdom. It was written as "On one side was Heaven, and then on the other Hell – well railed off from each other certainly, but rather too close for any comfort."

Example: He was too close for comfort. I don't feel comfortable with him.

Topsy-turvy

Meaning: In a reversed order.

Origin: Dates back from the early 16th century. It was first cited by Richard Eden in his book The Decades of the Newe Wolrde. He wrote "they see the houses turne topsy turuye, and men walke with theyr heeles vpwarde". He refers to things being upside down or the apex and the base were interchanged.

Example: She does everything topsy-turvy. I don't even understand how she does it.

Toss-up

Meaning: A situation where the results can go good or bad.

Origin: This idiom was first used in 1812. The expression originally came from the act of tossing a coin and guessing the side it would land on. This game is called "heads or tails" Most people would use this method as a strange way of making decisions on trivial matters.

Example: This toss up can go either way. Let's hope it favors us in the end.

Touch and go

Meaning: A risky or precarious situation

Origin: This expression comes from a certain situation when the ship is moving in shallow waters. Touch and go is an expression when the ship is traveling on shallow waters and accidentally touches a part of the seabed and reef. If the ship can avoid this situation, then it means that the ship had to touch and go. It was only in 1867 when William Henry Smyth's nautical dictionary, "The Sailor's Word-book" explained the phrase "Touch and go"

Example: It was touch and go; Mila doesn't know how to deal with it.

Tread tackie

Meaning: Drive or accelerate.

Origin: This idiom was from the shoes called "Tackie ". Although the origin of this expression remains uncertain, the word tackie has been used in many situations. Tackies are normally rubber-soled sports shoes but they can also mean slightly sticky figuratively.

Example: Parker treads the tackie before Roger could reach the finish line.

Troubled waters

Meaning: Difficult time.

Origin: This expression is taken from several other idioms. However, the phrase "troubled waters" often referred to stormy nights on the ocean, hence a difficult time for sailors.

Example: I am locked in troubled waters.

Turn the blind eye

Meaning: To refuse to acknowledge a known truth

Origin: This idiom first started after Horatio Nelson pretended not to see the signals of his partner Sir Hyde Parker during the Battle of Copenhagen. Nelson continued to push even though they were at a big disadvantage

Example: She turned a blind eye to what happened.

Turn the corner

Meaning: Pass a critical point after a difficult time; begin to recover.

Origin: This expression was coined because of the dangerous oceanic corner, namely Cape of Good Hope and Cape Horn. At both of these capes, the ocean waters would often collide, making it a difficult trek for seafarers. However, once they were able to turn the corner around these capes, sailors knew that the sea would be calmer.

Example: We all need to turn the corner to graduate with good grades.

Turn the tables

Meaning: Turning a position of disadvantage into one of advantage.

Origin: Originated between the 17th to 18th centuries in the game called backgammon. This expression came to be from a certain practice in playing the game. They turned the board around so that the player had to play what had been their previous opponent's position.

Example: She had turned the tables and she had a great advantage in getting the treasure.

Twist of fate

Meaning: Unexpected changes in the situation; unlucky turn of events.

Origin: This expression was taken from Medieval England when the Church held most of the power. That time, the Church taught the people that the strong belief of the people is the virtue of destiny. If they do something good or bad, they would rather credit it to the twist of fate than of the hard work or consequence of the person's doings.

Example: We were never ready for the new twist of fate.

Two peas in a pod

Meaning: Alike in both character and in looks

Origin: This idiom uses the allusion of peas inside a pod. If you look at these pees, they look exactly the same size, shape, and color. Figuratively, it talks about people who are very close and are often inseparable.

Example: The twins are like two peas in a pod.

U)

Under fire

Meaning: Being shot, or heavily criticized by the people.

Origin: This expression was first used in the early 1700s. It used to mean in the range of enemy fire. This expression doesn't have a clear root of how it came to be but it had been in circulation since 1800s.

Example: They were all under fire because of the plagiarism issue of the book.

Under siege

Meaning: To be under attack; criticized by people.

Origin: The word "siege" is taken from the Latin word "sege" which means seat in the 1200s. However, during the 1300s the definition of siege changed to describe a military attack caused by enemy forces.

Example: Soldiers were under siege when the other side released several airborne missiles.

Under the auspices of

Meaning: With the favor and support of a person or organization; under their patronage or guidance

Origin: The word auspice came from two different Latin words which are avis (bird) and specere (to observe). This expression was taken from a Roman custom where they consult a soothsayer or augur before going to war. This person would then observe the bird's flight, bird song, and even the entrails of the sacrifices before deciding the next move. Only the military chief would have access to augur's interpretation of the auspices.

Example: Under the auspices of my grandparents, I will partake in the upcoming debate this coming Sunday.

Under the rose

Meaning: In confidence; under a pledge of secrecy. archaic

Origin: In the past, it was dated that roses were an emblem of secrecy. This thought may have originated in Germany. Aside from that, there was a similar expression from the early modern Dutch. This expression also appeared in one of the state papers of Henry VII where he suggested that this expression was new and unfamiliar. This expression also has a Latin equivalent sub rosa and has also been very commonly used in English since the mid-17th century in this metaphorical sense.

Example: She swore under the rose that she will not speak a word about it.

Up a gum tree

Meaning: In or into a predicament.

Origin: Originally, this expression was first used in British English but was recorded in the USA in the 19th century. It was popularized through a song or dance of the same title.

Example: Mark has stuck me up a gum tree.

Up the ante

Meaning: To raise the cost or risk of an activity

Origin: This expression was taken from Poker. The word Ante was a Latin word that means before or in front. At the start of a hand, before any cards are dealt, players must place their bet at ante or upfront. As the game progresses, players can increase their ante. This causes the stakes to raise or "up the ante." This expression has been used since then.

Example: Darwin had to "up the ante" to make everyone understand the severity of the situation.

Up the pole

Meaning: Out of one's senses, mad; in difficulty

Origin: This naval idiom was taken from the idea of the ship's mast or pole. The pole is the part of the ship where most of the rigging often happens. One wrong mistake on the pole, everything in the ship falls down.

Example: Someone should go up the pole.

Up to scratch

Meaning: To be acceptable.

Origin: This expression came to be during the early days of boxing. During those times, boxers didn't use bells to tell them that the match had started. But rather, the boxing match started when you see the scratch line between the boxers. In the case of a knockdown, a fighter was deemed able to continue the match if he was able to walk up to scratch.

Example: It was her first time making cookies, they are up to scratch.

Up to the hilt

Meaning: Completely.

Origin: The image is that of plunging the blade of a knife deeply into something so that only the hilt is visible.

Example: Now we can exert our energy up to the hilt.

Up with the lark

Meaning: Up very early in the morning.

Origin: This expression was similar to the idea of Larks singing in the early morning in the 16th century. It was then used figuratively when referring to early risers as larks.

Example: She is up with the lark. She wants to finish her task earlier.

Upset the apple cart

Meaning: To create difficulty or cause an upset

Origin: Upset the Applecart is a position in wrestling. In the 18th century, the "apple cart" was a slang word used in wrestling. It means to circle the man's upper body. By doing so, they were able to throw the opponent's body down and put him in a difficult position.

Example: If you want a more challenging game, then upset the apple cart.

Us and them

Meaning: Expressing a sense of division within a group of people.

Origin: This expression comes with an underlying thought of us and them. "Us" referred to the people who have grievances against "Them" (usually people of higher class or power")

Example: Not everyone can be friends. Remember, there is a big difference between us and them.

Use your bean

Meaning: Brain; head

Origin: This expression stemmed from the idea that the brain looks like a bean

Example: Use your bean, you will be able to get the answer to this question.

Use your loaf

Meaning: Use your brain

Origin: This expression was taken during the First World War. Soldiers were stuck in the dig trenches and would hide there for days. However, there were times that they need to get out of the dig trenches and search their surroundings. To avoid being shot in the head, they would raise a loaf of bread to ensure that no one would shoot them.

Example: Use your loaf! We know you have the answer to this question.

Veg out

Meaning: Stop working hard; or to relax and take it easy.

Origin: This expression refers to the vegetative state of a human being. When a person becomes a vegetable, it means he no longer has the ability to do things on his own. Another definition of this expression refers to not working so hard and taking the time to rejuvenate.

Example: We can veg out on the couch and watch old movies.

W)

Wait and see

Meaning: Wait to find out what will happen before doing something.

Origin: This expression was first used in a speech by Herbert Asquith where he was asked about the rumors of a certain passage in the Finance Bill. To quote, Asquith said 'We had better wait and see.'

Example: Let's just wait and see how Jonathan will fix this.

Walk free

Meaning: Be released from custody without being thoroughly punished.

Origin: This expression was often associated with people who got out of prison but did not deserve to be there to begin with.

Example: He walked free, innocent, and without needing to post bail.

Walk your (or the) talk

Meaning: Suit your actions to your words.

Origin: This expression is the variation of the"walk the walk" and is frequently used to refer to expressions like 'He can talk the talk, but can he walk the walk?'

Example: Our company aims to provide quality service to our clients. It is our duty to walk the walk for them.

Walking on air (also, floating on air)

Meaning: Very elated and excited.

Origin: The phrase dates back to the late 1800s. It was often referred to the feeling of someone floating when they are very happy.

Example: She looked to be floating on air when we broke the news to her today.

Walking the plank

Meaning: Ultimatum or deadline to resign or stop

Origin: This expression was inspired by the ultimate punishment in the 1600s. Sailors that were accused of a crime were forced to walk off the end of the plank and drown. This practice was often used by pirates.

Example: Gina is walking the plank after everything had happened today.

Warts and all

Meaning: Including features or qualities that are not appealing or attractive.

Origin: This idiomatic expression was inspired by a request by Oliver Cromwell where he requested the painter Peter Leny. He wanted Leny to paint all the tiny details on his face including warts and all.

Example: For you to love yourself, you need to accept every inch of yourself, including warts and all.

Wash your dirty linen in public

Meaning: Discuss or argue about your personal affairs in public.

Origin: This expression dates from the early 19th century in English; a similar French expression about "linge sale" is attributed to Napoleon.

Example: I told Mara not to wash their dirty linen in public; people may think badly of their family.

Wash your hands of

Meaning: Disclaim responsibility.

Origin: Inspired by the act of Pontius Pilate who washed his hands before condemning Jesus Christ to death. The act of washing your hands is a ritual asserting that you are innocent.

Example: She had washed her hands of the possibility of ruining the events.

Water under the bridge

Meaning: Used to refer to events or situations in the past that are no longer important or a source of concern.

Origin: Likened to the water passing under the bridge over time. It referred to the idea that so many things have already happened prior to a particular event.

Example: She had forgiven her father. Everything was now water under the bridge.

Way forward

Meaning: The only way to succeed; the positive influence in a person's life

Origin: This expression's origin remains unknown. However, it is said to date back during the Old English era where the word future means towards the future. The word way refers to the path that leads to success.

Example: This job fair is the way forward for many individuals who are looking for jobs.

Way to go

Meaning: Used to express pleasure, approval, or excitement.

Origin: The expression is apparently an abbreviation of 'That's the (right) way to go!'

Example: Great job! That's the way to go!

Wear your heart on your sleeve

Meaning: Show all your feelings and emotions

Origin: This expression was inspired by the Medieval jousting matches when men would wear the colors of the women that they were courting. Hence, they wore their heart" on their sleeves.

Example: It is easy to know how you feel. After all, you wear your heart on your sleeve.

Wet behind the ears

Meaning: Inexperienced on the field

Origin: This idiom was likened to the birthing process of farm animals. When calves and kids are born, they are all covered in blood and fluids.

The mother often licks the babies but it's always the patch behind its ears that is the last part that dries.

Example: My sister was wet behind the ears when she first started her business.

Which side of the bread is buttered

Meaning: To be cognizant of where one's interests lie in a given situation

Origin: This expression first appeared in Proverbs by John Heywood. This expression was inspired by another idiom which is to "butter up". It is likened to the idea of which side the butter is spread by the person eating. Butter is considered something valuable in this idiom.

Example: We need to know which side of the bread is buttered. How will we know how to proceed if we don't know who to go to?

White elephant

Meaning: Holiday gift exchanges that are more impractical and useless.

Origins: This idiom originated from a legend. In the past Siamese kings would usually give white elephants to their subjects who betrayed or displeased them. However, this gift proved to be burdensome for their subjects. White elephants are expensive. Aside from that, they can't use elephants to work.

Example: Stop Buying unnecessary things! You are keeping white elephants at home.

White paper

Meaning: Official report or guide: Concise or complex information of changes

Origin: This expression was originally a British term. This expression was famous because of Churchill's White Paper. This paper was an official and accessible document. It was only then in the latter years that the word "white paper" has been used in many businesses, especially in the field of e-commerce and technology.

Example: We have the white paper ready for our upcoming discussion.

Wild goose chase

Meaning: Wasting resources on working or finding something that doesn't exist.

Origin: This expression was originally taken from a horse race called "Wild Goose Chase". The race involves several horses chasing the main rider who was a predetermined distance away. The horses on the ground would have that wild geese formation when you look at it from the top.

Example: We hope that she isn't leading us into a wild goose chase.

Win hands down

Meaning: Win easily with very little effort

Origin: This expression originated from horse racing. A jockey needs to remember to keep a tight rein on his horse and encourage it to run. But when the jockey is way ahead of his competition and would loosen his reins down. He will be able to win the horse race without raising his hand on the reins. Hence the expression, "win hands down."

Example: It was expected that Victor would win hands down in the Grand Prix Finals.

With bells on

Meaning: They wouldn't miss it

Origin: This expression dated back to the early 1700s by peddlers selling wares. To avoid Indian attacks, peddlers would muffle the bells on their horses but would unmuffle them once they reached their destination.

Example: I'll be at your party with bells on.

With forked tongue

Meaning: Untruthfully or deceitfully.

Origin: This image was likened to the forked tongue of the snake. In the traditional sense, snakes are also symbols of treachery and deceit.

Example: Many of us often talk with a forked tongue to protect ourselves from pain.

Wolf in sheep's clothing

Meaning: Someone who is pretending to be something they are not, usually to the detriment of others

Origin: This expression was cited in the Bible in Matthew 7:15. Jesus warned the people about the false prophets dressed in sheep's clothing who are just waiting for the time to corrupt them.

Example: I want you to be careful of this person. He looks like a wolf in sheep's clothing.

Word of mouth

Meaning: Oral communication; Spoken words used to convey information

Origin: This expression was dated back to 1533. It was first cited in the Oxford English Dictionary where it was defined as "the act of speaking and passing the information from one person to another in the form of speech."

Example: The final result of the contest was spread through word of mouth.

Worm in the apple

Meaning: Something rotten

Origin: The idea behind this expression is not really based on the actual apple but with Apple Incorporated and the bugs that cause the devices to malfunction. This expression was an example of an allusion of a worm inside the apple, slowly eating its inner parts.

Example: Believe it or not, he was the worm in the apple.

Worth your salt

Meaning: Good or competent at the job or profession specified.

Origin: This expression is taken in the context that Roman soldiers were paid a salarium which was literally translated as 'money to buy salt'.

Example: Hopefully, he is worth the salt. I expect to see my grades go higher this year.

Y)

Yes man

Meaning: A person who always say yes or agrees with everyone in the crowd

Origin: This expression was first used in Rome. Julius Caesar was furious at his council because they kept denying him the correct answers. Because of this, Caesar killed all his lawyers.

Example: Noah is a yes man. I never heard him disagree with anyone at all.

Yoke around one's neck

Meaning: A fatiguing burden.

Origin: The word "yoke" is an Old English word that means "to join together." A yoke is characterized by a heavy wooden collar that is fitted on a draught or draft animal. The yoke is attached to a plow or cart that the draft animals will be pulling. Figuratively, yoke is being referred to as the burden that one is carrying.

Example: Her current condition is the yoke of her parent's neck.

You can run, but you can't hide

Meaning: You can try to escape but will eventually be caught

Origin: This expression was first coined by the boxer Joe "Brown Bomber" Louis. In one of his fights in 1941, Louis fought Billy Conn, who was a lighter and faster boxer compared to Louis. Louis was able to knock out Conn in the 13th round. Years after, Louis still being the champion, Conn challenged him to a rematch. Announcers knew that Louis almost lost in his first bout with Conn and asked how he would be able to win against his 'hit and run" strategy. Louis had responded, "He can run, but he can't hide". Louis was able to knock out Conn in the 8th round of their second bout, making him still the champion.

Example: You can run, but you can't hide, I'll still catch you in the end.

You scratch my back and I'll scratch yours

Meaning: To do someone a favor if they do one for you

Origin: This expression first originated in the British Navy. In the 17th century, the punishment for being disobedient, drunk, and absent was often severe. One of the punishments that the sailors would undergo is being flogged with a cat-o-nine tails. Sometimes, they were tied to the mast and flogged with another crew member. If a crew member is tasked with flogging the punished sailor, they would deliver the lashes lightly. The hope was that if they were on the receiving end of the punishment, they would get the same light treatment.

Example: If you scratch my back and I scratch yours, it will be a beneficial thing for our business.

Young blood

Meaning: New member who can provide new ideas for the organization.

Origin: This expression was believed to be taken from African-American culture.

Example: We have a young blood who has recently joined the team.

Young turk

Meaning: A young person who is eager to reform the current society.

Origin: This expression was originally taken from a group of people called Young Turks in the early 1900s. The Young Turks were composed of the three Pashas named Mehmed Talaat, Ismail Enver and Ahmed Djemal who were the youngest members of the Turkish Nationalist Party that led the Turkish Revolution in 1908.

Example: Mila is a Young Turk with big goals for our society.

Your salad days

Meaning: Era of one's inexperience or immaturity.

Origin: This expression was taken from Shakespeare's "Antony and Cleopatra". Cleopatra was commenting on her relationship with Julius Caesar, stating 'My salad days, When I was green in judgment, cold in blood To say as I said then!'

Example: During my salad days, I don't even know how to use the oven!

Your ship has come in

Meaning: When one becomes rich and successful.

Origin: Dating from the mid-1800s, it was known that people used to invest in making ships. Many ship owners in this era believed that they could make money by having a ship that would help them recoup the money they invested. Investors would not see the ship for years or if the captain brought back some treasures. However, if the ship came backfilled with jewelry and valuables, then you could say that the ship had come in.

Example: Your ship has come in! All your hard work has paid off.

Z)

Zero hour

Meaning: A time when a crucial decision or essential action must be taken: (literally) refer to midnight, or 00:00

Origin: This expression was inspired by the German phrase "Stunde Null" which is translated to zero hour. This idiom came to be after Germany's surrender during World War II on May 8, 1945.

Example: It is the zero hour. We need to decide on this matter.

Zero tolerance

Meaning: Strict application of rules and does not tolerate bad behavior.

Origin: This expression was often used in the military. It is used to describe situations that come with serious offenses and punishments.

Example: I have zero tolerance for people who don't listen well.

Zip your lip

Meaning: To stop talking; To stay calm; To stay hush; To remain secret or silent

Origin: This expression was taken from another expression "button your lips". In the past, people used buttons to fasten their clothes. But with the invention of zippers, the expression changed to "Zip your lip."

Example: Please zip your lips! I can't think properly.

Zonk out

Meaning: To fall asleep very promptly

Origin: This expression was synonymous to the expression 'knock out". This expression gained its popularity around 1940 to 1950. It was only in the 1960s when this expression was used in many printed forms.

Example: He immediately zonked out as soon as he laid his head on his pillow.

CONCLUSION

Idiomatic expressions are the bizarre but well-loved expressions that we all use in our native language. Learning their meanings and origins will help you understand the evolution of the English language throughout the years.

Whether you are learning the English language or simply looking for the origin of these eccentric expressions, we hope that we were able to lend a hand with this book.

Thank you for sticking with us all the way to the end! We'd love to hear what you think. If you have comments, questions, or suggestions about this book, please let us know by sending us an email at support@ myenglishroutine.com. This will help us to enhance our books and provide you with better learning resources.

If you wish to learn more about the English language and its cultures, do visit us at www.myenglishroutine.com. We are always working to give you useful content.

And so with this, we say goodbye. Keep learning English!

Thank you!

The My English Routine Team

Your opinion counts!

If you enjoyed this book, please consider leaving a review on Amazon and help other language learners discover it.

Scan the QR code below:

OR

Visit the link below:

https://geni.us/b3SxCl

Printed in Great Britain
by Amazon

38345821R00145